TAKE
NOTHING
FOR THE
JOURNEY

Als letztes von der Ferne liegt dein Haus:
Wer du auch seist.

Rainer Maria Rilke

Your house is the last before infinity,
whoever you are.

TAKE
NOTHING
FOR THE
JOURNEY

MEDITATIONS
ON TIME AND
PLACE

Donagh O'*Shea* OP

DOMINICAN PUBLICATIONS
TWENTY-THIRD PUBLICATIONS

First published (1990) by
Dominican Publications
42 Parnell Square
Dublin 1

and

Twenty-Third Publications
185 Willow Street
P.O. Box 180
Mystic, CT 06355

Photographs on pages 4, 58, and 116: the author.
Cover photograph: Austin Flannery.

Cover design: Banahan McManus

Origination: Dominican Publications
Printed in the United States of America

Dominican Publications
ISBN 1-871552-1

Twenty-Third Publications
ISBN 0-89622-444-9

Library of Congress Catalog Card Number 90-70420

Contents

For my sister Rita
and
my friend Eppie

I thank my Dominican brothers and sisters
who read the manuscript of this book
and made valuable suggestions,
especially
Eppie Brasil,
Vivian Boland,
and
Paul O'Leary.

Introduction

All good books, it is said, are books of travel. Regrettably, it does not follow that all books of travel are good books.

This book is the story of a journey, one that falls somewhere between an exploration and a pilgrimage.

An explorer does not know the goal in advance; a pilgrim does — or thinks so. When asked by friends what this book was going to be about, I was always at a loss and could only say: "it will be about insides and outsides." I had to explore the meaning of *houses*. All my life I had been dreaming of them, sometimes almost nightly. I knew at some level that they were about intimate space, or what we call interiority. And I knew that the search for their meaning was likely to open out and become a search for intimacy with God. That gave it the aspect of a pilgrimage.

Modupe, a small boy in French Guinea, found a map of the Niger delta and brought it home as a gift to his father. To his dismay the father was deeply offended. "Maps are liars!" he shouted. "The things that hurt one," Modupe wrote many years later, "do not show on a map. The truth of a place is in the joy and hurt that come from it. I had best not put my trust in anything so inadequate as a map, my father counselled.... I had belittled the journeys he had measured in tired feet."

There are many maps of the spiritual journey, and most of them are useful, but they were never meant to be substitutes for the real journey to God. All maps are abstract and have to be tested on the road. I took to the road to get away from maps!

After ten years in St Dominic's, Ennismore, a busy retreat centre in Cork, I was weary from overwork and was afforded the luxury (or the necessity) of a sabbatical year. I chose to spend the first three months living in a tent in different parts of Ireland that held special significance for me. Many themes emerged during those months, clustering around two basic realities: time and place; and so I have subtitled this book Meditations on Time and

Place. These themes weave themselves constantly in and out like the strands of a rope.

I am tired of the use of the microscopic 'now' in popular spirituality. It is all right in itself, but when it is mentioned to excess it becomes extremely thin; it is too *abstract*, too remote from everything we mean by time. It is a perfect match for the abstract 'centre'. What can 'centre' mean if it is not associated with all the warm centres of being that I have ever experienced? It can only mean a mathematical point, with "position but no magnitude".

It makes little sense for us to try to disown time and place, since God has leaped into human time and place in the Incarnation. These are the structure of our reality. They are being put beyond our reach, and I am trying to claim them back.

Part One

1

"The eternal silence of those infinite spaces fills me with terror," said Pascal. The infinite spaces he spoke of were God's immensity and the creature's nothingness. I understand him a little back to front tonight. As I look up at the stars I reflect that the twentieth century sees instead the immensity of the created world and the nothingness of God. From where I lie, the galaxy seems after a few hours to overreach all passing emotions. The mediaevals called it the Way of St James, a touching pretence that it was only a larger neighbourhood; but naming it so cannot have done much to reduce the sense of its immensity. At any one time I can see two or three points of light moving: they are our contribution, artificial satellites trying to look like stars. From here they look like stars, but from *there*? I cannot begin to imagine *there*. But I am not, like Pascal, filled with salutary terror; I am empty and dislocated.

I have been lying beside my tent, and now I crawl inside it to recover a sense of proportion. Philosophers may speak of human reality as *Dasein* ("being there"), without qualification. I am not up to it. The best I can manage is a sense of being *here* — a sense of place, always particular places, habitable places. I am for houses, for nooks and crannies, for corners and cloisters and every kind of enclave and enclosure, natural or made by human hands; for interiors that do not smother, for huts and hermitages that look out, for rooms with a view. I make my own word for it: I am for *Hiersein*, for *being here*.

When you think about it, a tent is a kind of diaphanous house, thin-skinned, whimsical, offering slight protection. It fits in a small bag that can be carried in one hand; yet it is able to create a sense of inhabitable space. It creates a real interior. (Out of what? I ask when I see it folded). It gives one a sense of being protected from immense exteriors (protected by nylon?). Interiors are subtle realities and do not always need brick and stone for their construction. Perhaps the snail's sense of being protected by its shell is just as illusory, and just as real, as the inner space of this tent.

I am on pilgrimage to no one place but perhaps to the meaning of place, to *Hiersein*, to interiority, to intimacy (which literally means *depth*). I am tired beyond words, needing rest and solitude. In this pyramid-shaped tent I intend to live for some months; I have no wish at present to meet the Creator of the Universe: that is too much cloth for a tired man. But I do want to draw near to the Creator of all intimate spaces, and to the one who "pitched his tent among us."

2

Inches from where I lie, the wavelets of Lough Leane are making low sounds, regularly spaced like breathing. I love to pitch this tent as closely as possible to water. These sounds convey no urgency, make no demands; they are far removed from the world of telephones and doorbells. Even the chiming of the priory clock carried a hint of accusation. It measured time mechanically and not by human purposes. Its pitiless consistency made it appear a higher law. I gave my life in trust to the greatest killers: telephones and clocks; and they handled me unkindly. We allow these two to seem more real than everything else in the world. We live looking over the shoulder of everything before us. Things far away are allowed to be more real than the immediate: the 'tele' in telephone means 'far', and it was the same instrument, some say, that gave us the word 'phony'! Yet in spite of these associations of unreality the language of the telephone has embedded bits of itself in our speech: "I have your number" means "I understand you ... " How sinister! But here by the lake I have no number, and time is marked more humanely by the small waves.

"Nothing puzzles me more than time and space, yet nothing troubles me less, as I never think about them." I cannot recall who wrote this, and so I attribute it along with all such unclaimed baggage to the Italian writer, Ben Trovato! Time and space are the overarching frames of our existence, and unlike Ben Trovato I am both puzzled and troubled by them. I am in flight from them but also in search of them. I am in flight from mechanical time and in search of human time. I am in flight from imprisoning space and in search of intimate space. I am at once a refugee and a pilgrim.

3

The September night is long but no sleep comes. I get up and sit at the mouth of the tent. There is an awareness of a sea of time stretching ahead with no articulations in it but day and night. What a long night! Till now I hardly knew that night existed! I settle down to wondering if I have ever in my life experienced day and night as natural phases. They (and their different parts) are usually experienced as *institutions*. Evening, for example, is a collective dream of later-on, a fantasy about rest and freedom, harking back perhaps to school-days; someone called it "the shock-absorber everything rests on." Night is not really night, since it no longer puts an end to day. But on this pilgrimage, day and night will show themselves, I hope, in a new way. There is no doubt that night has fallen now on Lough Leane. The lake's face reflects starlight, and this scant light conveys the deepest sense of darkness. It has not the closeness of pitch darkness; it leaves a sense of distance, making darkness visible. I have to live with this darkness and not seek to impose distractions on it. It is something essential; darkness is always said to be *deep*. It has a velvety quality that seems beautiful as I become used to it.

Darkness is enchanting; it is like a desert where all parts are the same. Or it is like being under water: you sink into it and it swallows you. (Nature wisely protects us from too much of it, giving only one night at a time.) It is the perfect condition for deep meditation. The superficial differences between things are faded out and darkness shows you the heart of the matter. Night is for silence and rest: it is for when all is said and done. And when all is said and done, you see how little you know about anything. Yet this could be a blessing: to know *about* the world is not much

The word *about* is like a wedge driven between you and the object of your knowledge. That wedge does not drive the world out; it drives you out of the world. You are on the outside, cold and nervous, hoarding information like gold. But in darkness you are one with the world; you are on the inside; it includes you like a vast room. Yes, night is the time for meditation.

There is a tradition that sees God not simply as light but as darkness too: "translucent darkness", said Dionysius; "a silent hovering darkness", said Henry Suso; "an ineffable darkness", said Tauler and he quoted Proclus with approval, "a divine darkness, tranquil, silent, at rest, and out of reach of the senses." You could scarcely endure the thought of God if he had nothing to do with darkness. There would be no bridge between him and some of the deepest things in your own nature. Seeds consent to sprout only in the darkness of the earth; in broad daylight they wither. The heart is fruitful like the earth, and needs darkness to enfold new life. Meister Eckhart paraphrased a verse from the Book of Wisdom: "In the middle of the night when all things were in a quiet silence, there was spoken to me a hidden word."

4

Long past midnight I am still sitting at the mouth of the tent, welcoming the darkness and listening to the hushed sounds of night. In the dark the other senses come to life, especially hearing. This is a more intimate sense than sight. Sight is detachment, observation; and the English language has an absurd bias in its favour: we even go so far as to say, "I see what you are saying!" But hearing is a kind of communion.

I read with enthusiasm many years ago (but I recall it now with greater sobriety) that at the birth of modern science in Renaissance times there was a conscious choice of sight over the other senses. Galileo wrote, "I hold that there exists nothing in external bodies for exciting in us tastes, odours and sounds other than *sizes, shapes, numbers*, and *slow* and *swift motions*; and I conclude that if the ears, tongue and nose were removed, then shape, number and motion would remain but there would be no odours, tastes or sounds, which apart from living beings I believe to be nothing but words." Sight, in Galileo's world, is the sense to rely on; it tells you how the world would look even if you were not in it. The world is outside you, and you are an eye. This way of relating to the world became second nature and continued through the centuries. The Newtonian world was a strangely *silent* one. Language itself was turned into visible lines, as in a library, and even God was not allowed to speak. He was the silent architect, and in the eighteenth century he was further reduced to a "Force'.

See what happens when Galileo pulls off your ears! You can no longer believe in the God who speaks. Nor can you praise him or even curse him, because Galileo has also stolen your tongue!

In contrast to this, a Zimbabwean friend told me that the Shona language has a bias towards hearing: "I hear sadness, I hear joy, I hear a pain." There is more to the world, she said, than meets the eye.

I recall that in Zen meditation it is recommended to half-close the eyes. This is a sensible practice: not staring and not blindness, not broad daylight and not pitch darkness. There is something right about Milton's "dim religious light" — though ironically he was blind. Most people prefer candlelight to electric light when they pray: it does not obliterate darkness; it respects the shadows. When you are deep in thought you instinctively half-close the eyes, as if to say: "For a while let me exist from inner resources."

It is like closing the door (or the half-door!) of one's house against too much public life.

Here in this darkened lakeland there may be spoken to me a secret word.

5

"In the middle of the night there was spoken to me a word, a secret word." I brought just one of Meister Eckhart's ninety-nine sermons with me on this pilgrimage; it is a sermon on this text. At home I have a thousand books, but here I have not enough light to read even these ten pages. It is better so. I could light my lantern, but it would be only a clinging to the habit of turning night into day. Eckhart was not speaking of a written word, and besides, I know the words of this sermon almost by heart. What a strong compulsion to *see* words! (to see what he says!) I am to *listen*; and here at the lakeside everything helps me simply to listen. The longing for God that is born in the heart of such listening is, in Tagore's words, "the longing for the one who is felt in the dark but not seen in the day." Feeling and hearing are intimate senses. I must learn to recognise "the soul's most secret place ... where no image ever shone in."

I am finding it a hard discipline: Listen to every word that is not said. Listen for silences. I have become insensitive to the power of words because I hear and see too many of them. Yes, the mind has its ways of relieving this congestion. It ceases to pay attention. Good ... Yet not so good! Inattention becomes a habit; I lose the knack of paying attention. I need to fast a little to regain an appetite. So I don't say to myself, "don't listen to words." I am already a past-master at that. I say, "listen to silence." And I discover this: because silence seems empty of content I cannot place myself in relation to it, and therefore I cannot place myself outside it. It is a world I enter, not a world I observe. Silent people bear this out: they seem to carry a world with them, while the unsilent always seem to be scurrying in search of one.

Though I am not usually afraid of darkness, there is a sudden nervousness now. Why is darkness frightening? It is visual silence; and silence of any kind takes away your distractions (at least the outer ones). Then you are left with the self and you begin to see how readily you have been finding your identity in these distractions. Darkness is frightening because it lets one experience the self in its nakedness. But then there is the flight to inner distractions. Memory supplies conversations from the past. It is necessary to listen to these too, if only to slip free of the plot. And when you listen carefully you hear repetitions: you hear the pleading or the explanations or the anger. These have to be listened to with the non-attachment of silence. It is an arduous task to drag oneself into the present, the place of no roles, and to sit down in darkness: the outer darkness of this lakeland and the inner darkness of not-knowing. I recall the Meister's words: "There is nothing so unknown to the soul as herself."

"In the darkness a word, a hidden word." It is hidden even from oneself. You enjoy inner space, but such enjoyment is not necessarily meditation or prayer. You know how to settle down like a broody hen to enjoy the peace, but we have been told that there is a peace the world cannot give. It will be in you but not of you. Prayer is always in faith, and faith is dark knowledge. It is dark, and it is knowledge. If it were simply darkness one could ignore it; it would be unrelated. But it is a kind of knowledge and it lures you on.

There is no moon tonight: no sign of tomorrow — for moonlight is tomorrow's light.

6

Lying now in the tent, you wait for sleep to quench your last spark of sense. "In the darkness and silence, there was spoken to me a word." It is a word spoken long ago, yet waiting still to be spoken. You heard it in childhood, and you are waiting to hear it still. You found God, yet you are to seek him forever.

This much I know about seeking: most of it is self-seeking. The mind seeks peace, an end to conflict, a pillow to rest on. Can lazy searching find God? The mind loves to search idly as a way of escaping from itself, and it calls this a search for God! I will tell you what it is: it is a self-seeking escape from self, a pitiful floundering in opposite directions at once.

And yet ... and yet.... Despite everything it may not be a bad beginning or a shameful thing. A child perceives its mother first as a source of comfort and food, and only later as a full human person; but mothers find no fault with this. Why should you think God less motherly? Why should there not be *stages* in the approach to God? Children are often tough on smaller children, but adults regard them all benignly. Perhaps God has more tolerance of our early steps and crude stages than we ourselves have. God is not only the transcendent One; he is intimate to all things, all persons, all times, all places — to all fumbling and groping and vague searching. He beckons and we follow sleepily. We hear his call because he is intimate, but he is calling us to transcendence. He breathes or speaks or beckons and we follow blindly.

"In the middle of the night, a word; it came like a thief by stealth." When you search for God, are you searching for something to add to yourself? Will finding the truth be an experience of entering into possession of something? We are told that it is more like dispossession. God comes like a thief in the night. He ransacks our house, said Tauler. You are to learn detachment. It means something subtler than wresting things from your own grip (you would simply grip them with the other hand!). It means cooperating with the thief in the night, letting him steal the silver. Soon he will steal your last spark of sense, and at last your life.

Have no fear, God will search for you....

The last lines of a poem by Baudelaire often come to keep company at the very end.

> *Je vais me coucher sur le dos*
> *Et me rouler dans vos rideaux,*
> *Ô rafraîchissantes ténèbres.*

> (I shall lie on my back
> And roll myself in your curtains,
> O refreshing shadows!)

The small light of consciousness is fading from the world. In the Land of Winter. According to your word. In peace....

7

> *Wenn am Gebirg der Morgen sich entzündet,*
> *Gleich, Allerheiternde, begrüß ich dich;*
> *Dann über mir der Himmel rein sich ründet,*
> *Allherzerweiternde, dann atm ich dich.*

Goethe

> (When morning catches fire on the mountains,
> At once, All-Gladdening-One, I salute you;
> Then the sky grows pure and round above me,
> And, Lifter-of-All-Hearts, I breathe you.)

I awoke to the piercing sound of birdsong, startlingly close. During those moments while the mind fumbled out of its unreal world the sound entered without a name, with no interpretation, and it was the purest sound I have ever heard. A blackbird had perched on the tent, just over my head, and its sharp music brought me to my senses. When Thoreau heard a bird singing at dawn he would say, "There is one of us well, at any rate."

The world looks grey in the early morning, and after washing in the lake I am glad to sit here in the tent, to think and pray. The outer world has withdrawn and lost its mystery; like us it does not look its best in the early morning. The tent looks small and pitiful in the unflattering light, looks as if it were nowhere, as if it should not at any rate be here — surprised like a snail on the path.

Lifter-of-all-hearts, lift!

8

Sitting inside the tent in the early morning, the flaps closed, I dream again of inner spaces and question their meaning.

I remember the loneliness of some houses I have lived in, and their inner disconnections. And I also remember the house of my childhood, "a Being of warmth I think; at heart a house of mercy."

I remember old houses in which, as Eliot said, "there is always listening, and more is heard than is spoken." And at the other extreme I remember an ultra-modern cocoon-house in which I once lived alone for a week. It was in America ...

Coming from a country that the ancient Romans named the Land of Winter, I was new to high temperatures Fahrenheit. I wished I could at least translate them into Celsius, but I could never remember the formula.

The house had an elaborate burglar-alarm system that made me nervous of opening even a kitchen cupboard. There was also air-conditioning, and there were screens on every door and window to discourage insects from entering, and a bug-zapper to deal with them if they did. They should not come hither, and I should not go yonder to that place of suffering, for a great chasm divided us. The piped music was interrupted by an announcement that the temperature outside was 95 degrees Fahrenheit.

I knew the temperature, but I didn't know the heat. I knew *about* the outside, but I didn't know the outside. Knowledge had become information. I was a Peeping Tom, impotent but curious. The house satisfied perfectly the disturbing definition, "a machine for living in", and I began to understand what the American teenager shouted down to his mother when there was a power-cut: "Mom, my room has stopped!"

One afternoon I decided to escape temporarily from the cocoon — if only to prove that I was capable of independent existence. I walked for hours in the heat, strengthened by the need to prove a proposition. But I was conscious that I was somehow on the wrong scale: roads, distances, signposts, even buildings were all designed for motorists, not for pedestrians. I proceeded like a small insect for another hour and then crawled back to my cocoon.

In the middle of the night I awoke to the maddening sound of a mosquito. He was a plucky one who made his way through all those technological defences. He died in the early hours of the morning of August 18th, by *Time* magazine.

9

But here beside Lough Leane the balance of inner and outer conditions is level. Some ants and earwigs seem to consider the tent their home. As time goes by I come to accept this with as much grace as I can manage. One has to allow oneself to be at the mercy of the outside world, in some sense. A perfection that is achieved at the cost of complete isolation is not real. Within this isolated 'inner' we would create another trivial inner and outer: the same dialectics of *I* and *non-I*, of *mine* and *not-mine*, would still be at work, but in relation to trivialities. I have seen one or two monasteries where this is so. If there is to be an outer, it may as well be a real outer; otherwise the outer will be my brother, or even part of myself.

Once upon a time a sailor was shipwrecked and washed ashore on a desert island. He lived alone there for many years and built himself a village, which included a little church. Later he built another church at the other end of the village. The years went by and he was eventually rescued by a passing ship. As he showed the captain around his village he was asked, "Why this second church?" "That," he replied, his face hardening, "is the church I don't go to!"

There will always be the *non-I*, the other. The *non-I*, initially, is the friendly space that surrounds and protects the *I*. There are very many philosophers who think of it as the universe at large, making believe that they knew the universe before they knew the village — or the house or the room, intimate spaces. Better a real I and a real room than a reduced I (a spectator) and a universe. What kind of relationship can a spectator have with a universe? Can one imagine any *stages* in such a relationship? — any slowly widening circles where intimacy is enlarged as one becomes capable of it? The thought of an oversized world, a universe, frightens people into decreasing intimacy, insulated from all surroundings.

Descartes, who is called 'the father of modern thought', wrote: "I assume that all the things that I see are false. I persuade myself that nothing has ever existed of all that my fallacious memory represents to me. I consider that I possess no senses. I imagine that body, figure, extension, movement and place are but the fictions of my mind. What, then, can be esteemed as true? Perhaps nothing at all, unless that there is nothing in the world that is certain." He goes even further than Galileo and closes his eyes. Of course he still hopes to be in touch with the world, but through the mediation of intellectual knowledge. The million relationships that we have with the world assure him of nothing; nothing is accredited unless it be on the mind's terms.

Why such craving for certainty? Why such a need to have it on one's own terms? Why such timidity? Is it not very neurotic? Better a house, a hut, a cave (or even a tent) that I *can* live in than a universe that fills me with fear and suspicion.

I must not isolate the self, then, from the world (this would be a false immanence or intimacy), nor must I try to comprehend more than I am able (it would be a pretended transcendence). I must learn to live in intimate spaces and find there the keys that unlock successive doors to real transcendence. The house, that primordial symbol of the self, has windows and doors: it is not shut up in itself, nor is it open on all sides. It looks two ways: it looks in and it looks out.

In the months that lie ahead of me, these abstract thoughts — bare branches — may bring leaf and fruit of knowledge.

10

I have spent most of the day walking, and I was drawn this evening towards a small ruined house, the empty shell of some family in the distant past. I sat in its ruin for hours and meditated on houses.

To meditate on houses is to meditate on one's own being. It is to go backwards and forwards in time, as we do when we scan our own lives. Houses not only *have* history, they *are* history: when we meditate on them we always return to the first house, the house of our childhood.

The place of my first inhabiting was a small thatched farmhouse in north Cork, so changed now that its essence seems no longer there. People made fun of the townland and its odd, philosophical-sounding name, Beeing. Its remoteness made it difficult to explain where it was, and this always seemed like an inability to give a proper account of oneself. So for many years a certain shame of origins weighed heavily, like a coat that is out of fashion. I saw nothing special in Van Gogh's cottages until I saw something special in that farmhouse. By then I had long since ceased to live there. But to return to it in dreams is a perfect homecoming.

It seemed like an organic being. Nothing was quite straight or right-angular; walls, floors, ceilings all followed soft lines. On the outside the walls had received coats of whitewash to a depth of more than an inch. Many ancestors had whitened them, laying down lime like coral, the alluvium of generations: the house was *made* of time. Chickens would sometimes peck at the walls when they needed calcium for their eggshells, and their concentrated efforts on one patch revealed that the house had once been red! I remember feeling darkly that those chickens had gone too far this time. It must have seemed that they had drawn blood!

A tiny window peeped out from the attic at floor level. Lying on the floor, staring through that window, I spent endless hours daydreaming. It was the essential experience of *inhabiting*, of nesting. The house under its thatched roof was a loving protector, but it never stifled curiosity. On the contrary, the smallness of the window increased curiosity. Over everything reigned a great silence of the countryside. There were no engines or motors of any kind. On fine summer days the window lay fully open, as if the house were panting a little in the heat. In winter the rain fell silently on the thatch.

In the attic were three hats that belonged to the three generations before my father: a bowler, a top hat and — the oldest — a hat of no discernible shape that was worn by my great-great-grandfather. To this day the metaphor of roots says little to me; I think of the dead generations in terms of hats! Like skulls, they once enclosed living minds but now they were silent, even solemn, in their abandonment. I would climb into the attic and wear them: how stiff and dry they were! I felt a special affinity with the oldest one; it was less formal than the others — and so too, I thought, must have been its owner. I was the youngest of his descendants, and all time was suspended between us. It was my first conscious aware-ness of paradox: a distant presence. To this day I cannot experience any depth of consciousness without that attic and its silent ghosts making their presence felt.

By returning to the house, and within the house to the attic, I bring all of the self to reflection and prayer. That house is at the heart of all one's experience of interiority. The road to transcendence begins in childhood in the intimate spaces where the self first learned inhabiting.

It is almost night now, and I return to the tent as to a fragile home. Sitting, thinking, praying within it, I am also in the house of my first inhabiting; and between these two small spaces all time is suspended.

11

Day has brightened over the waters, and the far trees like a great gathering wave are yet motionless. The only sounds are the songs and noises of birds: urgencies and significances that are happily lost on me. Time will stir slowly today.

The road is open before me, and I want to travel westwards as far as I can go: towards the Blasket Islands, the western edge of Europe. The journey is a short one, fifty miles. But it is more an inner than an outer journey, and distances in the inner journey are not measured in miles. "It is not physical but mental steps that bring us closer to God, since he is everywhere," wrote St Thomas Aquinas (with perhaps too much disjunction), *non passibus corporalibus sed affectibus mentis.*

The function of inhabiting is only half the story. One also has to leave the house. Having spoken of the need to go into the house of the soul, Tauler added, "Next the soul must go out; it must travel away from itself, above itself."

The soul must go out. Otherwise its interiority will be false; it will be a flight from the outer world rather than a resonating with it. It must travel away from itself, above itself. Otherwise the challenge and vigour of the opposite will not be felt. The door must be opened, winter must be welcomed, the opposite embraced.

Irish weather makes no promises, since it never knows its own mind. The day looks unsure of itself, trying one thing and then another. If I am to live a while with uncertainties the stage is correctly set. And my means of transport adds its own uncertainties. It is an antiquated Honda, compensating for its mechanical nature by its great age and its soft purr. I regard it with something like the affection that Monsignor Quixote, Graham Greene's version of Don Quixote, had for his battered old Seat 600, his 'Rocinante'. It is several years since I did any repair work on it, and I hardly think of it any more as a machine. It seems to be party to the search for essentials, for it has lost almost every inessential part, such as drive covers and side covers; and it stands there like a donkey in ragged honesty, humility and patience. Like Sancho Panza, it only lacks a tail to be a perfect ass.

It takes a leisurely hour to fold up the tent and set my belongings on the Honda for the uncertain journey.

12

It is difficult to leave this beautiful place ... It seems I will always have trouble with leaving, with going out. But there is no choice: one must cross the threshold, the place of ambivalence, the axis of turning-in and turning-out. The inner and outer meet there, and one has to pass with knowledge from one world to the other. What an abundant reality to meditate on: the *threshold*! How satisfying its ambiguity is! Everything is there. It has the resonance of our two opposing needs: to be hidden and to be visible. The same door is wide open and firmly locked; it invites and it forbids. Think of the spectrum of feelings associated with opening and closing doors! If you were to give an account of all the doors you have opened and closed, all the doors you would like to re-open, said Bachelard, you would have to give an account of your whole life.

What resonance there is in all ambiguity! And how impatient we are to be rid of it! It is the moment when two meanings are held close together, like seashell and eardrum, and for an instant the world is not flat. Each echoes the other, the inner ebb and flow hears itself as ocean. The soul must go out: not into the flattened world of Descartes but into a world that resonates in the soul's interiority.

13

A road, a mile of kingdom. I am king
Of banks and stones and every blooming thing.

Patrick Kavanagh

Time moves differently on the road. It stands still like the air when we are still, but when we move it seems to rush at us. Of course it is we ourselves who are rushing. Time is oneself. What do I give when I give my time? I give myself. We hide this from ourselves when we measure time by an abstract arithmetic. It becomes a separate reality, a possession rather than the substance of our own existence. We count it as we count money.

I read that the Nuer, an African people, have no word for time, and they are unable therefore to think of it as something that passes, that is caught up with, that is saved or wasted or fought against. They do not imagine that they ought to co-ordinate their activities with an abstract passage of time; their only points of reference are the activities themselves, which are generally of a leisurely nature.

This was true also, in large measure, of Beeing, where I grew up. People said *harvest-time* for *autumn*, *after dinner* for *afternoon*, *cow-time* or *milking-time* for *evening*. I remember a porter in the nearby hospital who used to patrol the wards a few hours after visiting-time was over, ringing a bell and cajoling the last of the visitors to leave: "You may as well be moving on now; it's cow-time!" Before our fixation on mechanical measurement of time there was only "a time for sowing and a time for reaping ..."

The Honda has forsaken also the counting of miles, the speed-ometer indicating a perpetual motionlessness. It has entered into the mood of this pilgrimage and prefers to saunter along, disdain-ing all arithmetic. Robert Pirsig claimed in *Zen and the Art of Motorcycle Maintenance* that "the motorcycle is primarily a mental phenomenon," and that "the study of the art of motorcycle maintenance is really a miniature study of the art of rationality itself." Pshaw! I don't agree! I find it a dangerous idea. My Honda is beyond all that. This morning, as if to shrug off such nonsense about rationality, she refused to start. "Mental phenomenon"! If she were that, then this breakdown would be a mental breakdown! No, I would never accuse her of such a thing. She was just a little exhausted and needed to rest. I parked her on the road, beyond the bushes, where there was a fresh breeze, and I returned to take my leave of Dunrower and Lough Leane.

She started, of course, and now two hours later we continue to saunter westwards. She seems entirely at ease with the tradition of sauntering, a word that comes from *Sainte Terre*, the Holy Land. It is a word that holds some memory of the contemplative loitering and dawdling of millions of pilgrims down the Christian centuries. Galileo loved those qualities called 'primary' — size, shape, number, swift and slow motion — because they were measurable. Imagine a guest whose only interest in your house lay in measur-ing everything! You would suspect him of planning some kind of raid. And raid they did, these measurers. Some scientists (or rather their admirers) seem to like the word 'raiding' as a description of what they do: raiding the universe for its mysteries, raiding the earth for its minerals. Yes, the world is divided into measurers and saunterers. And these times I am on the side of the saunterers. "I have a ring with a hawk and a butterfly upon it," wrote W. B. Yeats, "to symbolise the straight road of logic ... and the crooked road of intuition: 'For wisdom is a butterfly and not a gloomy bird of prey.'"

14

My new dwelling-place is a patch of ground only a little larger than the tent and one pace from a stream that runs into the sea at Dunquin. A few feet to the rear there is a high protective bank where blackberries are already promising in early September. It is a perfect enclave, and the Great Blasket lies in full view three miles across the sea to the west.

A deep vein of nostalgia in my nature brought me here. That steep barren island with its deserted village stands in my mind for everything that has been lost. In the final thirty years of its life the island community produced several writers of great stature, and sixteen books of autobiography, story and verse. It was as if they rushed to tell the world their story before they expired; "for the likes of us will not be seen again," wrote Tomás O Criomhthain; "*beimid sínte go ciúin — agus tá an seansaol imithe*," wrote Peig Sayers, "we will be stretched out quietly — and the old world is gone." Around the turn of the century they numbered about one hundred and fifty people, but because of the hardship of life on the island and decreased numbers (there were only twenty-two in the end) the remaining inhabitants moved to the mainland in 1953 and their village fell into ruin. "You can always tell an islander," a neighbour told me, "they have a far-away look." I saw an old man standing for hours on the cliff-top, looking across the sea at his deserted island home, the Western Island, *an Oileán Thiar*.

Small shells of houses cling like barnacles to the great bulk of the island. Or they seem like creatures that struggled heroically once upon a time to free themselves from its grip, for they remain embedded up to their roofs on the steep side. From this distance the village seems tilted up for our inspection, framed above by the round back of the island and below by dark cliffs and darker rock-gullies. The distance in space — making the village seem just beyond reach of any help — combines with the distance in time, to create a picture of heart-breaking sadness. Robin Flower, who loved the island and its culture more than most, wrote: "The world has turned to another way of life, and no passion of regret can revive a dying memory."

The village seems sunk in a double abyss of space and time. Stripped of the thousand signs of life that inhabited places send out — shouts of children, patches of cultivation, chimney-smoke — it lies still, like a father's dead body, bereft, beyond reach of all help, displayed in its essential solitude.

All things, including the self, hover in that double abyss. Here, in sight of this dead island, I am to draw up all my forces against too much nostalgia. I have to learn to love to the right degree the essential loneliness of all things. I have to contemplate with equanimity ruined houses, centres of being that lived once but now no more.

Even the woodgrain of a table or a floor has the power to set me dreaming about the past: what year was this, this line? What kind of summer, what gales and winds, what birds sang here and children climbed, what people came and went? I am to conquer the nostalgia of houses, to let them be places of *present* inhabiting, without losing the loving associations of the past. For this I sit here and look across the sea.

How am I to find balance between opposite excesses: too much feeling and too little? It is useless to force a balance; the effort would create further imbalances, like awkward movements in a curragh. One has to wait and let it come. Perhaps balance will find me.

15

Night descends slowly and the only sounds are of sea-waves expiring, like the generations, on the sand below and the small gurgling sounds of the stream beside me. The island darkens in the distance and sinks into a deeper mystery. Things of the past are out of reach of our help. There is nothing we can do for them; they are purely for contemplation. Their speech is almost pure silence and we can speak to them only in that language. It is a strange language, with little or no grammar. It has nouns only, but they have one verb-like quality: a past tense. I am happy to live with nouns for a while; I have lived too much lately with verbs. But I must ease the grip of the past tense, without forsaking it. Sitting in the tent I watch the island disappear, minute by minute, shade by shade, into the night.

Long after nightfall I continue to sit and look out into the darkness. Thoughts stir in the mind. Our life is stretched out over time, and as time perishes we perish. Excessive nostalgia is a wish to *contain* our life — like listening to this stream beside me and wanting to gather it all up. It is a refusal to let time pass, to let the stream flow. The stream knows something that I have to learn: it is not a stream unless it flows; contained, it is a stagnant pool. In the darkness I can hear it. It is a stream of sound; it is music. What would a piece of music be if all its sounds were simultaneous? It would be a glut, a mouldering excess.

Jonathan Swift imagined an island where some of the inhabitants 'enjoyed' everlasting life. Far from being a gift, however, it was a horrible fate, for they aged like everyone else, but without hope of release or rest. At a hundred they were feeble creatures, and sad because all their friends were dead. At two hundred they were utterly miserable and had become strangers to the human race. At six, seven and eight hundred they were a curse on the earth.

Swift got his story from the ancient Greeks. Aurora, the

goddess of Dawn, fell in love with a mortal youth named Thanatos (which means Death). She besought Zeus to grant him the gift of everlasting life, and he agreed to her request. A few years later she realised she had made a mistake when she saw the signs of age on Thanatos. She ought to have asked for everlasting youth, not everlasting life.

These stories are a comfort, but not much. What is their comforting moral? Death keeps you young! I heard of a man who was terrified of old age, and so he asked God to allow him to remain at the age of thirty-nine for the rest of his life. God answered his prayer: he died that night!

In the pitch darkness I lie inside the tent and turn my face to the sound of the stream that flows down beside me to the desolate sea.

16

Today I am to set foot for the first time on the Great Blasket. 'Great' is a relative term: it is greater than the other Blaskets but it is still a tiny island, three miles long and less than a mile wide. As adventures go, this is on an absurdly small scale. Yet even the shortest journeys can have some of the magic of heroic voyages of discovery, because travelling is always a personal matter. Without the eye of the traveller what would a travel tale be but a geography lesson?

Christians through the ages have loved to travel. They had the perfect excuse: the Lord had sent them! And they felt entitled to look at everything along the way. An Egyptian monk of the sixth century, Cosmas of Alexandria, reported: "The Monoceros, or Unicorn, I cannot say that I have seen ... but the hog-deer I have both seen and eaten." That was surely a reliable reporter, and his tests the ultimate in verification. But Christians are not alone in their love of exploration. A thousand years earlier, Herodotus reported on the wildlife of Egypt: "There is a sacred bird called the phoenix, which I have never seen except in a picture, for it seldom makes its appearance." These two travellers show that what is not seen is often more interesting and gives greater proof of veracity than what is seen. And so (in theory at least) there need never be such a thing as an uninteresting journey.

However, for every Cosmas or Herodotus there is an Antoninus of Piacenza. He visits the Holy Land in the year 570 and 'discovers' in Tyre that "life there is very wicked"; he then checks Sidon and finds it also "very wicked". Like many travellers he tended to see only what he had read about. Yet he saw or imagined it with such engaging naïvety that one cannot help but follow him. "In the city of Diocaesarea was the chair in which the Blessed Mary was sitting when the angel came to her.... Three miles farther on we reached Cana, where our Lord was at the wedding; and we reclined upon his very couch, upon which I, unworthy that I am, wrote the names of my parents."

Antoninus may not be the most reliable authority on matters of fact — he saw the world with his heart and his imagination — but I would prefer to have him as a travelling companion than all the generations of editors of *The Blue Guide*. I try to imagine what his innocent eye would have seen on the Great Blasket, and what wonders he would have reported of Seán Eoghain and Peig and Peats Sheamuis and all the imaginative people who lived there in the lamented past.

17

What was once said of Ireland may be true at any rate of the Great Blasket: that she is a fruitful mother of genius but a barren nurse. The barrenness of the island is startling when you come near. From sea-level there is nothing to be seen but bare rock; and the green slopes are hidden beyond the cliffs. "We lived in the shelter of one another," wrote Peig Sayers, quoting the proverb, "*Ar scáth a chéile sea mhaireann na daoine.*" Her words could bear a vivid literal meaning on these wind-whipped slopes. *Scáth*, shelter, must have been a basic word in the vocabulary of the people who lived here; there is not one tree on the whole island.

I wished I could be alone, but noisy companions dissipated all the romance of stepping ashore. Yet they are part of my cure, these wake-goers, for they represent what we loosely call reality. They will not allow me to tint this ruined village with the sepia of Romanticism. Here will be no ruined castle against a storm-tossed sky, no hopeless passions or impossible aspirations. The accent is local, earthy, real; there is nothing to encourage the remote gaze, especially not the cold Atlantic to the west.

As we climb towards the village I am struck by the smallness of everything. There is a special pathos about the path, now partly overgrown, that leads steeply upwards to the cluster of little houses. It brings Tanaka's words to mind:

> Beaten and buffeted
> By the rain and wind,
> An ox drags his load
> Past and is gone,
> Leaving only
> Wheel tracks in the mud
> And the sadness of things.

The ruinous houses seem so tiny and defenceless. They need no defences, of course: they have the indifference of death about them. Sad thresholds, forever associated with childhood, with the contentment of homecoming and the excitement of visitors, have no welcomes left. Hardest of all to look at are the hearths: no-one will ever say again, "sit up to the fire." The language of those hospitable people, the *glan-Ghaoluinn*, is silent. These little houses were built by the people who lived in them. "Nobody had to hand me so much as a stone all the time I was at work on it," wrote Tomás, "and I roofed it myself." In that respect these houses are like birds' nests, built from within, the bird pressing out with its own body. And now, more than most ruinous houses, they seem like the dead bodies of the people who inhabited them.

18

I climb a higher path and sit to watch the village and the White Strand and the sea beyond. *Ein Wesen der Ferne,* Heidegger called the human being, a creature of distance. We are the only creatures who are able to look at anything from a distance: we have distant horizons.

The great Romantic poet Schiller distinguished between "naïve" and "sentimental" poetry. (These were not disparaging words in the eighteenth century.) When it sees our natural life as harmonious with our spiritual life, poetry is "naïve"; when it sees a contradiction between them it is "sentimental". This distinction was later rephrased as Classic-Romantic. The Romantics in their decadent phase made much of the sentimental, cultivating the sense of loss, tragedy and distance, and an unlimited self-absorption. Descended from Kant, that subverter of objective knowledge, they curled back on themselves like cut wire. They celebrated imagination, and held up nature as a mirror to themselves. And of course they gave nostalgia a bad name. Certainly they saw distant horizons, but those horizons were loose and dreamy, consisting of fog instead of land. Sitting above the village I am aware, yes, that we have distant horizons; but I am more aware how difficult it is to see anything at all with clarity.

Has naïvety no horizon? Can we see anything from within? Or is clarity always the outsider's view? Certainly there is a tendency to fall back on the view from the outside and trust it absolutely. It is assumed that if you want the truth about love, for example, you must not ask a lover but a psychologist; if you want the truth about religion you must not ask a religious person but an anthropologist; if you want the truth about some movement or ideology you must not ask someone who lives within it; no, you must ask a sociologist. The outside view is given such authority that its least syllable is thought to debunk the inside view. You reach absurdity very soon this way, because without the inside there is no outside. An outside view that took no account of the inside view would be knowledge of nothing, or it would be knowledge of something else — some general view of the world, some theory. But how do you get the inside to speak for itself? When it begins to speak, does it not become an outsider to itself in some sense? Was Tomás not already taking his leave of the Blaskets?

There is a famous photograph of Tomás standing at the door of his house, staring fiercely under his wide-brimmed hat into the camera. It comes to mind now as I look down on his roofless house, and it speaks to the questions in my mind. It says one word: *threshold*. He is standing at the place where two worlds meet, the inner and the outer, behind him his house, his history, his resource — his source. He faces outwards, stands before the world, speaks from his source. A purely outside view is empty horizon; and a purely inside view would perhaps have little or no horizon at all. The place where they meet, the threshold, is reducible neither to one nor the other. All viewing, all speaking, is from a threshold between inner and outer worlds.

On his own admission Tomás helped bring the culture of the Blaskets to an end. He read stories to his neighbours "and though they themselves had a lot of stories they lost their taste for telling them to one another when they compared them with the style the books put on them." The terrible 'objectivity' of the printed word! His friend Seán Eoghain was equally clear about it: "It's Tomás who has done it," he said to Robin Flower, "for he has books and newspapers and he reads them to me, and the little tales one after another, day after day, in the books and the newspapers, have driven the old stories out of my head. But maybe I'm little the worse for losing them." That he had no regrets is the saddest part, and it shows how vulnerable naivety is. It was Robin Flower, the outsider, who had the regrets. "The reality of the tradition is passing from us now," he wrote, "and I can only think that the world is poorer for its passing."

Sitting above the village, encircled by the vast horizon, I begin to think of the countless traditions that have died and are dying daily in the wide world. So much sinks without trace: houses, families, histories.... "Not people die but worlds die in them." Writing and reflection help to speed up the process; perhaps these are the ripeness, and after ripeness comes death. And so the cycle continues forever, like the turning of the seasons. Naivety, the inner view, is lost by being understood, for understanding is the outer view; then there is a new naivety, which will be lost in turn.... This is life, this is our dilemma, to be forever on the move to a kind of knowing that is shallower and thinner than experience, a knowing that shrivels its object.

No doubt it has always been so: Orpheus was leading Eurydice by the hand from the underworld, the deep; he had been warned not to look back at her, but his love compelled him: he looked at her and she disappeared.

Tomás stands forever at the thereshold, telling the story of his people; Orpheus perpetually leads Eurydice over the threshold of the underworld. All things strive and strive again for the bland light of day. But thankfully there is no perpetual day for us in this world, only a perpetual daybreak.

19

"How sweet it tasted!" My companions have assembled at the slip — some who soon had enough of the Great Blasket have been waiting here for more than an hour — and we set out for the mainland. Looking back at the island I am reminded of the Zen story about a man who encountered a tiger and fled in terror, the tiger after him. Coming to the edge of a cliff, he took hold of a root and swung himself over the cliff just out of reach of the tiger. The tiger snarled at him from above. Trembling, the man looked down and saw another tiger far below waiting to kill him. Only the root sustained him. Then there came a mouse who began to gnaw at the root. The man saw a luscious strawberry nearby. Grasping the root with one hand he plucked the strawberry with the other. How sweet it tasted!

Only passing things are beautiful. Their sweetness cannot be preserved. "Why am I passing?" Beauty asked Zeus, in Goethe's *Four Seasons*. "Because I make only passing things beautiful," answered Zeus. *Macht ich doch, sagte der Gott, nur das Vergängliche schön.*

The little boat rises and slumps with the waves when a rough wind catches us from the west. As I glance back I see that the island is withdrawing with vastly more grace than we ourselves can manage at the moment. It looks like a queen; it looks eternal. Then the awareness strikes me with great accuracy: it *is* eternal; it is we who are mortal. How things turn back on us! How the mind revolts! How meanings turn back to front!

I see a sizable opening in the mind, a thought that needs to be thought: nostalgia is about one's own death.

But that is not for now.

20

Il dolce far niente, the idle hour, is not always *dolce*, not always sweet. The excess of activity that made this pilgrimage necessary is still overflowing. My visit to the Great Blasket, despite the tranquillity of the island, stirred me deeply. It is necessary to learn

a new art: the art of climbing down. The stream that flows beside
my tent may teach me this too; it climbs forever downwards.

The tent, when I returned to it, looked puny and insignificant.
It too has its threshold, but my eyes were set on other thresholds
and other interiors. It is now late afternoon and I sit within its
space, knowing nothing but the necessity of returning to common
reality.

The stream beside me dashes purposefully to its destination —
to the ocean where all purposes and destinations become one. We
always speak of *higher* purposes; well, the ocean is a *lower*
purpose, a *deeper* purpose. This is a more restful image than
higher purposes. Every influence in our world sends us up, praises
higher intensity. Those expensive rockets to nowhere are the
culmination of modern culture and symbols of the way we think
we ought to live. I will sit by this stream and try to learn climbing-
down, try to learn deeper purposes.

I search in a pocket for my rosary. Recently this form of prayer
has become very meaningful for me. Something happens to time
when you pray this way. The string of beads has a beginning and
an end, and the end is the beginning. It is a loop and it creates a
'time-loop'. It is a circle, a perfect figure that needs to go nowhere,
and it suggests a contemplative pool, an image of the roundness of
the ocean, the *perfecta possessio* of eternity.

In Irish it is called *paidrín*; *paidir* means prayer, and comes
from *Pater noster*. It is a more essential word for prayer than any
other I can think of. Jesus said, "Ask the Father." If you put the
emphasis on *ask*, you get words like *pray, pregare, prier, beten* -
all of which mean *ask*. Or, as in Irish, you can put the emphasis on
Father — which seems a better idea.

I often invent my own 'mysteries', or rather I pick many more
than fifteen from the pages of the Gospels. This evening I want to
see the Lord 'climbing down'. I imagine him visiting one of his
favourite families, Martha, Mary and their brother Lazarus, to rest
after a day of heat and frustration. I see him asleep in the corner and
the others on tip-toe so as not to wake him. When you sleep you

almost resemble an object. Who and where and what is he when he is asleep? The Hail Marys are a way of measuring time. They are also pure atmosphere, mostly memory, and there is no need to concentrate on the words. If it seems a little drowsy, that may indeed have something to do with 'climbing down' and 'deep purposes'.

What happens to time when we pray like this? "I believe Bethlehem, Golgotha, the Mount of Olives and the resurrection to be truly in the heart of the one who has found God," wrote St Gregory of Nyssa. Prayer time seems to be quite different from clock time. It is in some sense an inner time: a time in which past and future are in the present, a time that embraces remembrance and hope.

21

It is evening and the falling darkness makes the world look smaller and closer in every direction. Time, however, seems vaster than before. Or rather it moves more slowly and therefore seems longer. I am disappointed to find myself checking the time very often. You have no appointments! Why does this habit cling?

A Hindu philosopher remarked that the clock was a Christian invention. Time is running out, the end is coming, there is no recurrence. (The hour-glass, I think, would be a better symbol of this kind of awareness; after all, the clock repeats itself forever.) The prospect of eternal recurrence is terrifying for Hindus; and so, the way to shock them into deep realization is to threaten them with just that. Christians, who generally enjoy life a little better than the average Hindu, are shocked in the opposite way: by the prospect of *not* recurring — by the once-for-all quality of life. This, the philosopher claimed, turns us Christians into the minute-minders we are.

It is true, we have often regarded time in the manner of misers, hating the loss of the years. Yet we also go to great lengths to waste time. We want it both ways: we want to squander and dissipate our treasure and yet, impossibly, we do not want it to diminish. If our time is us (as it is), then confusion about time is confusion about ourselves. We are afraid to live, yet we want to live forever.

I have found that I am never more conscious of the clock than when I have forgotten for a while the meaning of my life and have given way to dissipation. When one fails to understand something there is an urge to measure it. It seems that when other structures of meaning fall away, the forward march of the minutes is the only structure left.

In William Faulkner's novel, *The Sound and the Fury,* Quentin is about to commit suicide, when he takes his watch and breaks the glass, then pulls off the hands. "The watch ticked on. I turned the face up, the blank dial with little wheels clicking and clicking behind it, not knowing any better." The destruction of even this final structure symbolises the loss of all meaning. "I could hear it, ticking away inside my pocket, even though nobody could see it, even though it could tell nothing if anyone could." There is no past and no future: no history and no adventures. Not only Quentin's own life but every event in history has lost its meaning: "Christ was not crucified: he was worn away by a minute clicking of little wheels."

In other stories by Faulkner there is a reaching towards a different kind of time, called 'mythic time': the perpetual present of ritual. When ritual is performed, the past event becomes present again. This kind of time is not linear like clock-time; it is recurrent — even cyclical if the myth is related to the seasons or other natural processes. William Barrett related this to the primeval sense of time in Homer's epics. "The audience knew the story in advance; it was only a question what episode they might desire to hear.... The myth is thus perpetually present with them, renewed whenever the bard might appear.... The siege of Troy takes place again and again, and Achilles will pursue Hector around the walls of Troy forever."

Homer's world seems a long way from here and now, yet it was from listening to the storytellers on the Blaskets that George Thomson found the key to 'the Homeric question'. With his own eyes he saw what an oral tradition looked like when it was written down for the first time. He compared those two worlds, so distant from each other in time and place, and saw how each produced a literature that retained all the signs of a long oral tradition; the two kinds of storytelling, oral and written, were intertwined in a wholly distinctive way.

So many thoughts, books, writers filing past the mind.... They are like thoughtful visitors; and part of their thoughtfulness is that they know when to leave. But they have left behind them an atmosphere of peace and deep restfulness; perhaps this is what 'mythic time' feels like.

Mythic time: somewhere along here lies the answer to too much nostalgia. And somewhere along here there opens a path to contemplation.

22

The dust of dead worlds clings to thee,
Wash thy soul with silence.

That was a fleeting visit from Tagore. Now even he has gone, and there is a vast silence of night, made even more vast by the nearness of the stream's music. It resembles the sound of singing kettles long ago in the country of childhood, surrounded by friendly darkness. Imagine, beyond, what solitude the ocean must have in the night! Imagine, this night, the island's loneliness! Yet now as I look across to see its dark outline I know that the island lives and dies *in me*; it exists in mythic time, and lives and dies and lives again in every mind that remembers it. Tomás stands at his threshold forever, telling the story of every man and woman; Peig walks down the hill towards the village, she is suddenly gripped by the beauty of the island and the ocean; remembering her dead children she prays with every mortal sufferer, "Well I know your holy help, because I was often held by sorrow with no escape." Her prayer of that day lives forever; it is temporal and eternal, 'temp-eternal'.

There is no place for nostalgia: that is only a Romantic posture, a refusal to enter the human reality of history. In my being I enclose the Blasket ... and the night encloses everything.

23

In the Talmud it is written that all water has its source in the primordial river that flowed out of Eden; therefore when you immerse yourself in the ritual bath (the *mikvah*) you are renewing your link with Eden. As I immerse myself in this less ritual stream, its chilling waters are able, at any rate, to renew my link with Dunquin after a night of dreams. I fall to wondering if the primordial river was warmer than this stream, or colder. Warmth we associate with dreams and fancies, and we call reality cold. Eden, I think, was the place of dreams, like a womb or a feather bed. Welcome, then, colder reality! Better a little chattering of the teeth than idle dreaming!

By and by I am to have another immersion in reality when an elderly man approaches my tent from upstream. He is a local man and, as I am to discover, the owner of the tiny patch of wasteland on which I am camped. He displays the kind of surprise that a countryman displays on meeting you after he has watched you for miles. He stands beside me, looking away at the weather and discussing it with urgency. One always knows in such a case that the urgency is about some other matter. Now he comes nearer to his topic; standing in the same place but looking now at the ground, he inquires about myself; how long do I hope to stay? Fifteen minutes later he is telling me about some foreign students who camped on this very spot last year and never thought of paying a penny, the careless little devils! That's youth for you! This gives me every opportunity to reflect on my own comparative age and the better sense it should confer on me. After a decent length of time and much frowning on the defects of foreigners in general I begin to search my pockets for money. The bank-note I find there is an alarmingly big one, but who could stoop to mentioning fractions in such genial company? His practised eye takes in the colour of the note as I slip it in his pocket (for that is the proper etiquette) and his face lights up in a radiant smile. He begins to tell me about his poems and promises to bring me a copy of the latest one.

Soon he is taking his leave and heading towards another tent which has sprung up during the night some distance away. He is a genial old man, and his way of doing business is human and engaging. Tents are a sort of hobby with him, and lucrative in a small way, like picking mushrooms or snaring rabbits.

I miss his company, the old rogue, and I think about his bright smile and the money that put it there.

Money ... money. Mammon — God's greatest rival. Now that I think about it, water is a constant metaphor in the language of money. Why? They talk of liquid assets, frozen assets, currency, cash-flow, being solvent, flooding the market and floating a loan; even in the case of dirty money the metaphor still holds: slush funds and laundered money. It must be that money is useless unless it flows. When it is hoarded it loses all meaning, like blood that does not flow through the body or like stagnant water.

And time is money, we say. We save and spend it, like money. We are unhappy when we have not enough and still unhappy when we have a lot of it.

For all these, substitute the self. You save yourself, you cautiously spend yourself, or you give yourself away with abandon.

The stream will teach me wisdom even about this: its busy water, yes perhaps flowing out of Eden after all, will give itself within minutes to the vast Atlantic.

For the first time since this pilgrimage began I am beginning to find immensity thinkable.

When I look across I see a young man standing out beside his tent; and there beside him stands the poet, indicating with large gesture the beauty of the surrounding countryside.

24

"At a certain season of our life we are accustomed to consider every spot as the possible site of a house," wrote Thoreau. "The only house of which I had been the owner before, if I except a boat, was a tent," he added touchingly. He gives reasons for his "experiment" of living alone on the shores of Walden Pond, in a house built with his own hands: "I went to the woods because I wished to live deliberately, to front only the essential facts of life ... I wanted to live deep and suck out all the marrow of life, to live so sturdily and Spartan-like as to put to rout all that was not life, to cut a broad swath and shave close, to drive life into a corner, and reduce it to its lowest terms.... " Ouch! such *aggressive* verbs: *to front, to put to rout, to cut, to drive, to reduce*.... And from a hermit too! It comes as no surprise that his vocation to the wilderness lasted only two years. I once met a real hermit, a Camaldolese monk, who said, "God lured me in here to persuade me to stop running from him." He added nothing about cornering God, for God had cornered *him*.

It is near midnight now and the whole world is still. I am lingering at the mouth of the tent before going to bed. Some shrubs beside me are visible only as outlines of deeper darkness. Their outer world of twigs and leaves is plunged almost as deeply in obscurity as their inner world of roots. Everything becomes its own essence at midnight. Only the deepest movements continue, the heartbeat, the stream's flow and the eternal birth-movement of the sea. This is God's time; he chooses to *need* our darkness. "What good is light," said Eckhart, "if it does not shine in darkness?" God plays with light and darkness; he plays hide-and-seek.

It is the most essential of all games, hide-and-seek. Babies play it, without being taught; they bring it from God. If I want to know what God's joy is like, let me listen to a baby's laughter when it is 'found'. There was a Zen master who used to play hide-and-seek with children. He played with utter single-mindedness; once, he hid himself so successfully that he was not found for three days. God plays with utter devotion, hiding in darkness sometimes for weeks or even years. It takes two, at least, to play: I seek and God hides, I hide and God seeks. If one side gives up, there is no game.

This must be why Thoreau sounds so grim; he is not playing a game but mounting an assault. "The intellect is a cleaver," he explains, "it rifts its way into the secret of things."

As I leave my place at the mouth of the tent and withdraw into its interior, I know in my heart and soul that the real secret can never be assaulted; it can only disclose itself with joy.

25

"We came to two streams, the Jor and the Dan, which flow into one river and are called the Jordan. It is small where it enters the sea; it flows through the whole sea and runs out on the opposite shore." My unmistakable friend is back, Antoninus of Piacenza. He keeps me company at breakfast as I sit on a rock some fifty yards upstream from the tent. Two streams meet at this point; in memory of him I call them the Jor and the Dan, and I eat this apple in his honour. He is the right kind of company on a bright morning.

This place where the streams meet is surrounded by high banks and thick shrubbery, and it forms a natural enclave. It has become my favourite place for praying the psalms. Someone said once that Christianity is a very indoor religion. That is strange when you consider that Jesus lived with mountains, the sea and the desert, and claimed that he had nowhere to lay his head. These prayers were his, and they fit well with the outdoor world:

> You make springs gush forth in the valleys,
> they flow in between the hills,
> earth drinks its fill of your gift.
> There is the sea, vast and wide,
> with its moving swarms past counting,
> living things great and small.

There is a sense of immensity about everything this morning. Even Antoninus of the fanciful details shares in it; his great antiquity confers it on him: he wrote his account of the Holy Land around the year 570. He prayed these psalms on his journey, and they were as palpable to him as "the bench upon which our Lord used to sit with the other children," or "the book from which he learned the ABC." For the moment, immensity has lost its glaring, unfriendly aspect; it is a tender quality, a soft shadow partly hiding each thing; it is a touching naïvety, a dim radiance, unspeakable humility. The Father's immense love is partly guessed by every creature.

> The goats find a home on the mountains,
> and rabbits hide in the rocks.

The untold story, the shy fecundity, of each being is the Father revealed and unrevealed in it.

> You send forth your spirit, they are created ...
> you take back your spirit, they die;
> you hide your face, they are dismayed.

The psalms, as I have been taught, are the word of God. They are not simply my words, then. Does God have to tell me what to pray for? Yes ... yes. How well I know it! Left to myself I would never pray more than "Give us this day our daily bread." Not the poverty of my own heart but the richness of God's word must teach me what to pray.

Another immensity stretches before the mind: the vast throng of God's children. I am not praying in my own name alone but in theirs; we pray together as brothers and sisters of Jesus. The 'I' of the psalms is also a collective 'I', a 'we'.

> I will sing to the Lord all my life,
> make music to my Lord while I live

— even though I may not have a note in my head!

> I find my joy in the Lord

— even when I am tired and despondent.

> Out of the depths I cry to you

— even when I feel on top of the world. I myself may not be feeling great joy or sorrow at this moment, but I can be sure that thousands, millions, of brothers and sisters are. Many of them may not be able to turn their raw human experience into prayer, and may depend on me and others (in God's providence) to do so for them. In turn, they sustain me and make up what is lacking. The psalms are the voice of the whole Church and they take me beyond the limitations and the randomness of my own feelings.

Sitting here at the junction of the Jor and the Dan, I am one with everyone who has ever prayed these prayers. The presence of Antoninus has been like a balm; he has made me reflect that more people are cheated by believing nothing than by believing too much. My expensively bought dullness may be brightened by his imagination, so vivid that he smelled sulphur at Sodom and Gomorrah and saw, when the tide went out, "the marks of the army of Pharaoh and even the tracks of his chariot-wheels."

26

All day long I have done nothing but look at things: rocks, shells, insects, plants and above all the sea. Their tranquillity, their dim light, their deep humility is a source of healing for the spirit. Strange that it often takes the non-human world to restore our humanity — yet, when I think about it, it makes perfect sense; we are to be human *in* the world, we cannot be human if we sever links, however subtly, with it. When we divide ourselves from the world we are dividing our own nature. We divide ourselves from the world by *observing* rather than *contemplating* it. Someone called observing an act of aggression: as soon as you begin to observe (with all its connotations) you start measuring and counting.

A Japanese poet of the seventeenth century, Basho, who wrote a travel book with the wonderful title, *The Records of a Weather-exposed Skeleton*, also wrote this minute poem, a haiku, about a wild flower:

> When I look carefully
> I see the nazuna blooming
> By the hedge!

He does not pluck it, he does not give its scientific name; he *looks carefully*, he contemplates it. D. T. Suzuki contrasted this with a poem by Tennyson:

> Flower in the crannied wall,
> I pluck you out of the crannies; —
> Hold you here, root and all, in my hand,
> Little flower — but if I could understand
> What you are, root and all, and all in all,
> I should know what God and man is.

This kind of "understanding" is just as violent as the plucking: it *is* a kind of plucking. He has no care for the flower itself, he is interested only in the moral that he can extract from it. Suzuki sees this as typical of a Western way of looking at the world. However, my frequent visitor Goethe is able to go part way to restoring the reputation of the West:

> *Im Schatten sah ich*
> *Ein Blümchen stehn,*
> *Wie Sterne leuchtend,*
> *Wie Äuglein schön.*
>
> *Ich wollt es brechen,*
> *Da sagt' es fein:*
> *Soll ich zum Welken,*
> *Gebrochen sein?*
>
> *Ich grubs mit allen,*
> *Den Würzlein aus,*
> *Zum Garten trug ichs,*
> *Am hübschen Haus.*
>
> *Und pflanzt es wieder,*
> *Am stillen Ort;*
> *Nun zweigt es immer,*
> *Und blüht so fort.*

(I saw a little flower growing in the shade, luminous as the stars, bright as an eye. I wanted to pluck it, but it spoke in a tiny voice: 'Am I going to be plucked and to wither?' I dug it out, little roots and all, brought it to the garden of my lovely house and replanted it in a quiet corner. There it continues to grow and blossom.)

These three poems represent three ways we have with the world: the way of contemplation, the way of curiosity and a kind of middle way. And since we ourselves are part of the world, these are also ways we have with our own being: there is a contemplative attitude to the self, there is the way of self-destructive curiosity and there is the way of self-improvement.

The trouble with self-improvement (or self-fulfilment) is this:

the 'self' that tries to do the improving is the very self that needs most urgently to be improved. We would lay out the garden of our "lovely house", our self, according to our own taste; but that is the problem: our taste is in question. We would have everything under control; but that again is the problem: what does it all serve? I once saw a garden that was planted and cared for by a mathematics teacher, and it sometimes haunts me still. Daffodils stood to attention at arm's length from one another like soldiers; pansies lined up straight like little orphans in an institution; identical shrubs stood at either side like deans of discipline. Oh for a little anarchy there! — even a patch of nettles or briars, anything to relieve this planned monotony, this tyranny of self-will. (There is self-improvement of the sloppy kind too, but that is usually much more transparent.)

What vitality the unexpected brings! Every washed pebble on this beach has its own story to tell — and not only its own but the story of the planet. At the latter end it is also *our* story: stones have entered the human world of meaning. Like inflexible words themselves, they help us to picture the hard heart, the unfatherly gift, the immovable obstacle. But they are also symbols of stability and endurance, even eternity. In *As You Like It*, the Duke saw "books in the running brooks, sermons in stones, and good in every thing." Some scholar (or was it someone in jest?) claimed that this was obviously a corrupt text and that the original must have read: "stones in the running brooks, sermons in books ... " How that scholar would parse and analyse the world! How he would arrange it in rows, like the mathematical gardener! How he would eliminate all surprises! How he would stand with firmly shut eyes and ears and refuse to *contemplate* the world!

We live still in a mental world shaped by Kant, who made contemplation impossible in principle. All knowledge, he said, is discursive: the work of reason lies in deducing, demonstrating, distinguishing, comparing, relating, abstracting. "Reason acquires its possessions through work," he announced. He identified reason with what the mediaevals called *ratio*, and rejected the

function they knew as *intellectus*: the receptive or contemplative
side. Knowledge, he said, is work, "a herculean labour."

But what a relief, to give *ratio* a holiday and to live sometimes
by *intellectus*! What a luxury, a day in which to look and listen, and
to touch things without having designs on them! — without
working on them! It is one way to learn contemplation of God and
to unlearn the habit of interfering with his grace in our inner spirit.
Before he reached for his shovel Goethe was a contemplative,
"without any idea of looking for anything."

> *Und nichts zu suchen,*
> *Das war mein Sinn.*

I want to listen to the story of every object and not interrupt its
humble, whispered speech. I may catch an echo of God's voice.

Leave me now, Goethe, take your friends and enemies with
you, and don't forget your shovel. If the poet finds you here he will
lighten you by a pocketful of Gulden!

27

The sea, being boundless, is one of the few things in the world of
which there is enough for everyone. Its vast tranquillity tonight is
reassuring, its many treacheries can be forgotten. It stretches out
endlessly, tracklessly, like eternity itself. It breathes.

Sitting on this large rock for an hour or more, down at sea-level,
it is easy to fall in with the rhythm of the waves. For a long time
there is only the thought of the endless ages during which the
waves have washed these rocks; it is an annihilating thought and
there is a temptation to sink into a kind of 'sad shepherd' mood.
But the time for this indulgence is past. There has to be a new
awareness. *I* have not lived through those endless ages, I cannot
comprehend the sea, nor eternity, I cannot even comprehend a

pebble. Nor can anyone. Our life is short, we cannot wish we were as old as time itself, we have nothing to regret.... It is important to look into the right abyss.

The living breath comes and goes in waves, like the sea. The wave recedes to nothingness: there is nothing to regret.... No need to long for what has passed.... Give everything away.... At the end of the breath, nothing, perfect stillness. What freedom there is: to live *in* the world and not *behind* it ... together with countless beings. The wave returns, washing through the whole body.... Everything is received as a fresh gift ... because of the purity of emptiness....

"Whoever wants to receive everything must also renounce everything," said Meister Eckhart, "that is a fair bargain and a just return. Therefore, because God wants to give us himself and all things as our own free possessions, so he wants to deprive us, utterly and completely, of all possessiveness." The heart of all possessiveness is the need to control, the need to have things within our power. When our sense of "I exist" relies on this need for power and control, then our deepest relationship with the world is a power struggle. We are threatened on every side, and it is dangerous to relax even for an instant. It is even more dangerous to go to sleep, because when we wake up we may find that the world has changed and we are no longer in control of it. How could we find God in anything while we are in the throes of this neurosis? *He* will have to find *us*. He will find us and deprive us of all possessiveness, Eckhart promises; he will teach us the wisdom of giving up everything.

I discover, against all logic, that the way to breathe more deeply is not to draw more air into the lungs; that only causes tension and self-consciousness. It is to exhale a little more deeply than usual; then the inhalation becomes deeper by itself. The way to have more of anything is to give more away.

God is vast and fruitful like the sea or the air. There will be enough for everyone. I was told about a strange old man who filled his home with scrap metal, piling it high, year after year, till there was no space left but a path between the door and the fireplace. What a vivid image of the human mind! But God will deprive me of everything and I will think that my 'house', my life, is being destroyed. He is only making *room* — a word that means *space*, or even *emptiness*. "In return for my going out of myself for love of him," said Eckhart, "God will become my own, with all that he can bestow, as much my own as his own, neither less nor more."

It is dark as I leave the sea to return to my tent beside the stream. The waves continue to come and go as they have always done and will do forever. I have lived a while with the eternal sea, "endless and sublime", the beginning and the end of all rivers — moving image of the Alpha and the Omega.

28

In the middle of the night I wake suddenly though all is still. Darkness, the eldest of all creatures, holds sway in the world; and the mind is full of darkness. There may be stars out, for all I know. The thought occurs that they may be dead for thousands of years, for all I know, while the last of their light falls on us. Night has always seemed rich, deep and comforting, but tonight it is the very image of death and the void.

The thought that one is to give up everything is deeply disturbing when it begins to strike root. Since time falls away ceaselessly, every breath is in a real sense the last. Into your hands I commit my spirit, the breath of my body...my life. Can Nothingness look at a Christian too? "They give birth astride of a grave, the light gleams an instant, then it's night once more." Are we sitting after all with Vladimir and Estragon? "Adieu. Adieu. (*Silence. No one moves.*)" Another of Beckett's creatures, *Murphy*, took to spending "more and more and more time in the dark, in the will-lessness, a mote in its absolute freedom." They are cheerless companions, these spectres, these waifs. They are like tearful parodies of Eckhart and St John of the Cross, but tonight they have managed to get on the inner track.

There is nothing for it but to lie here in what yogis alarmingly call 'the corpse posture', that is, on the flat of my back. The phrase is much too accurate for comfort. How comfortably Chuang Tzu seemed to live with the Void! "In the Beginning was Void of Void, the Unnamable." But Beckett's novel of the same name, *The Unnamable,* is one of the saddest books ever written. "Only I and this black void have ever been.... I know my eyes are open, because of the tears that pour from them unceasingly." Unlike Chuang Tzu we are prisoners in the world of objects and actions, and escape from it will cost us everything. Hundreds of times I have read, "Blessed are the poor in spirit," but now when I experience poverty of spirit I do not call it blessed. Perhaps that is right: not I but the Lord calls it blessed. I live now *in* the world, *in* this experience, not behind it.

It is a great comfort to remember that St Thérèse of Lisieux, "the cherished child of the world," said startling things that one might have attributed to Beckett. "I cannot convey to you," she said to one of her sisters, "the darkness into which I am plunged.... It seems that darkness ... says mockingly to me: 'You are dreaming about the light.... Dream on! Rejoice in death which will not give you what you hope for, but even deeper night, the night of nothingness.'" So nothingness does stare at Christians too, and even at the greatest saints. She quoted Job's deepest act of faith and applied it to herself: "though he slay me I shall trust him." Thérèse is a welcome friend on this dark night. Eckhart, too, is a solace and a light — not a light that takes away the darkness but a reassurance that darkness is not dreadful. "Stand still," he says, "and do not waver from your emptiness ... Your being aware of God is not in your power but in his. When it suits him he will show himself, and he can hide when he wishes."

This is hide-and-seek, then.... But it is not such good fun as I thought! Perhaps when you lose control of the game it seems less

entertaining. I am beginning to see that there are deeper dark-
nesses than the kind velvety I so enjoy. To live with them I will
have to learn a deeper kind of laughter. Eckhart (and many others)
spoke of darkness and "unknowing knowledge"; "your knowing
must become a pure unknowing, and a forgetting of yourself and
all creatures." Am I a prisoner still in the world of objects and
actions? Will I have no intimate space, no house, no threshold?
What about mythic time? Are all my new thoughts to be swept
aside? Who could bear the thought of an immensity that destroyed
all particular places?

Night, which brings all creatures home, is saying tonight that
there is no home anywhere.

29

The shreds of a dream drift away like thin cloud as I wake. Only
one clear detail remains, a painting. There was a hatted figure
looking straight out, and a wide landscape in the background. I
turned the canvas around and saw that it was also painted on the
back: it showed the back of the man's head and a different
landscape, the one before him. The rest of the dream was a vague
awareness of the painted head turning different ways.

Is a dream the voice of God, as some claim, or just the child of
an idle brain? "Too flattering-sweet to be substantial," Shakespeare
suggested. In this case, at any rate, it is not substantial at all, it is
a two-dimensional picture. As I turn the picture over and back in
my mind this morning, I see it related to that question of Nothingness. Is there any place for a three-dimensional person to live? If
you were to give up everything, as Eckhart said, would you be real
anymore? Would you be no more than a slice of a person? And
would you exist any longer in real time? Would you not be trapped
in the timelessness of a painted picture? And how could you will

or do anything? The last line in each part of *Waiting for Godot* is: "Yes, let's go. *They do not move*." If you give up everything, is that what you get: will-lessness, apathy?

An Irish saying a *seanfhocal,* comes to my mind, an appropriate one for now: "You don't plough the field by turning it over in your mind." I have no answers; I will have to *live* with these questions today, *thinking* about them is not enough. If dreams are the voice of God he is a very questioning God! I am sure that a question is often more profitable than an answer: you forget an answer once it is given, but you have to live with a question. An answer is often a locked gate, but a question is an opening, a possibility. Through that open gate I must go — not with the mind alone but with the entire being. R.D. Laing managed to sound like a Zen master when he put this in words:

> As one goes through it,
> one sees that the gate one went through,
> was the self that went through it.

30

> I am a pilgrim on the earth;
> show me your commands.
> My soul is ever consumed,
> as I long for your decrees.

Psalm 118 always seemed to me like a large quantity of leavings; others had feasted here and left nothing but these bones. How could you pick any devotion from words like *precepts, commands, decrees, laws*? How could the psalmist, or anyone praying this psalm, be so enthusiastic about them for 176 verses?

"My soul lies in the dust." I can relate to that line. It was some fellow-feeling with dust that brought me to Psalm 118 this morning; but there is more dust here than I bargained for. Teach me the demands of your statutes.... Make me grasp the way of your precepts.... Give me life by your decrees. If that much law is needed to keep us in check we must be greater rascals that we thought! In fact that much law would *make* rascals of us, just as fences are only a challenge to schoolboys. What kind of religion is this that tries to keep us in pound forever? It sounds as passionless as Alexander Pope:

> The first Almighty Cause
> Acts not by partial but by general laws.

There seems to be no intimacy there — no depth. When they want to talk about God why do people use the word *law*? Human laws affect you externally, on the surface; and in the eyes of the law you are only a slice of a person: not a full-blooded human being but a 'citizen', a 'driver', an 'owner', and so on. What are you before God's law? Is there any place for a three-dimensional person to live?

The sea is calm this morning, "the unplumbed, salt, estranging sea." It is moved by laws you cannot touch or influence in any way. *Stand still and do not waver from your emptiness*. You are sitting again on your favourite rock (there is a homing instinct even towards rocks). All around you on this rugged beach, stones, large and small, lie quietly with gestures of renunciation. *Stand still and do not waver from your emptiness*. Prometheus unbound has nowhere to go, like a chicken too accustomed to captivity. Some passion — anger — would give energy, but *stand still*. There is no energy, even to waver, but *do not waver from your emptiness*.

"God cannot leave anything void or unfulfilled." Eckhart's words are like a promise. "God and nature cannot endure that anything should be empty or void." I recall some of the sparkling things I have read in books of holistic spirituality: be creative, be free, be joyful, be fulfilled. Eckhart does not say this; he says, "Do not waver from your emptiness and God will fulfil you." A superficial spirituality promises you everything without your having to give anything up. It promises you 'self-fulfilment', the wisdom of the snake eating its own tail, an illusion of infinity. Kierkegaard spoke of "the desire to anticipate eternity," like the impatience of children. "But eternity is *now*," we shout. *Now*? At this hour and minute on your watch? *Now*, the exclamation of your inability to wait for anything? No, it will be God's time, God's 'now', and you must learn the wisdom of waiting.

The sea knows the times of its ebbing and flowing.... *Got wirt und entwirt*, said Eckhart darkly, "God becomes and unbecomes." Another translates it "waxes and wanes". Perhaps he ebbs and flows like the sea. When thoughts of him enter the mind they rise to the top; they appear to be 'important'; then I think I am full of God. But it may be that the nearer one comes to God the fewer the thoughts one has about him. By showing me emptiness he is showing that he is deeper than the rise and fall of human thoughts; he seems to us to rise and fall, but no human scale can measure him. He is measured by himself; like the sea, he follows his own law.

"Lord, how I love your law." The long psalm begins to appear in a new light: a song of praise to God who is akin to the ocean and the mountains and the wind.

> Your justice is eternal justice
> and your law is truth ...

The ocean of his being is the *only* place where three-dimensional life is possible! I am to dive headlong — as far as I have courage — into the ocean; then he will teach me to swim and laugh and to experience the deepest joy.

> Let your love come and I shall live,
> for your law is my delight.

31

"Humanity does not pass through phases as a train passes through stations," wrote C. S. Lewis: "being alive, it has the privilege of moving always yet never leaving anything behind." This is very clear, perhaps a shade too clear. You should leave *everything* behind; only then is it yours to take with you. Or conversely, it is only when something is really yours that you can leave it behind. It was only when the Blaskets became the substance of myself that I got them out of my system. I am no longer weakened by nostalgia for what can never be restored. But the inner Blaskets come with me: through them I have gained a little insight into the riddles of time and place. Threshold and mythic time seem useful images, but I do not know whether or how they bear on transcendence, that is, on God's immensity. *Solvitur ambulando*; it will be made clear as I go along.

The poet visited me last night with a gift of lobster claws for my supper, or rather he hailed me from across the stream and threw the claws over. They were already cooked; he only had to give instructions on how to get the meat out with the handle of a teaspoon. I will miss his visits and his notable good nature. I had a sense, last night, that it was time to leave Dunquin and the Blaskets, and I took my leave of him. I have spent ten days here. Today I set out for Kilmallock, to live for a few weeks beside the ruins of a mediaeval Dominican Priory.

The Honda, the "mental phenomenon", starts easily this time. Any sensational developments in her innards she thoughtfully keeps to herself, like a discreet friend. All my worldly goods are loaded on her back: the tent, an inflatable mattress, sleeping bag, pots and pans, a tiny gas-stove, a few books, and dangling at the back a battered storm-lantern such as farmers used before the age of electricity. Riding cautiously through the village of Dingle, I am reminded of Nietzsche's madman who "lit his lantern in the bright morning hours, ran to the market place and cried incessantly: I am looking for God! I am looking for God!" If I were to do that among these placid people I doubt that I would get as lively a response as he did. A young man had time to examine the lantern as I waited in traffic; then he looked at me and said, "I see you are keeping up with the times!"

Part Two

32

"Let us wander around Ireland," wrote P. W. Joyce in 1869, quoting John O'Dugan of five centuries before: *triallam timcheall na Fodhla*. If he were to wander around Kilmallock today, O'Dugan would not lose his bearings, I think. Entering the town by the mediaeval Blossom Gate I have the impression of a town whose main buildings, with one or two exceptions, are mediaeval ruins. Almost directly in front of me is the collegiate church of Saints Peter and Paul with an early round tower incorporated into it; further along, astride the main street, is the enormous bulk of John's Castle. Here I stop to look around, for I know that the object of my search cannot be far away.

There it is, visible through a gateway, standing apart on level meadowland, only a hundred yards from where I stand: the thirteenth-century priory. The first glimpse is like a shock: it looks so clean, so handsomely compact and peaceful that it seems a pity it should stand empty of community. But there is no mistake; it is indeed a ruin, roofless and grey with age. To my great delight I see that there are no barnacle-like tombstones around it; here it will be possible to live.

Now that my journey is over I must remember the discipline of 'climbing down'. I take plenty of time to find the best place to pitch the tent. It is a patch of ground a little way from the priory, beside the river called the Lubagh. Having put everything in order I sit on the ground and look across at the ruin, not wanting to invade its privacy too suddenly. I heard once that the Sioux Indians regarded every object as a place where the Great Spirit had stopped: trees, rocks, animals, mountains — all were places where the Spirit had stopped and rested on its flight. The Spirit assuredly rested here too, and still rests.

The Lubagh is little more than a stream meandering past my tent; its name, in fact, means 'curving'. Time will move slowly here, like a lazy river making its way without haste to some distant sea.

33

I am filled with curiosity as I make my way across the Lubagh to the priory, but I would like to think it is not empty curiosity. "It is impossible for anyone who has had even slight experience [of monastic life]," wrote Patrick Leigh Fermor, "not to feel, at the sight of empty monasteries, a sorrow sharper than the regret of an antiquarian." The tower of St Saviour's (for that was the name of this priory) is taller than the usual squat towers of mediaeval Dominican priories, and it has been partly shattered on one side by lightning. "But we have only to close our eyes for a second," continued Leigh Fermor, "for the imagination to rebuild the towers and the pinnacles and summon to our ears...the sound of bells melted long ago."

Entering the ruined church by the main doorway I am made vividly aware that I am a few hundred years late for the echo of Gregorian chant, the rising clouds of incense and the sound of urgent preaching. There is only a much diminished interiority; the roofless structure seems to hold nothing in — almost everything has slipped from its hold. There is no shadow, no darkness. The doorway, that magical place of transition, no longer has a solid door but a gate. The outside has firmly established itself on the inside: the tension of inner and outer is slackened in the entropy of death. It is a comfort, however, to notice that there are no tombstones on the inside either. Human beings have no monopoly on death, though tombstones always give the impression that they have. Spared the repetitious details, I will be able to contemplate death in itself.

I hear rapid footsteps on the gravel and a very small boy appears. He is a self-appointed guide with a serious speech impediment, but he manages to convey the essential information: a guided tour would cost me ten pence. It was a castle, he explains, as he leads me around; beyond that door were the prison cells and over there was where the prisoners were tortured. There follows a long story, very little of which I can make out, told with enthusiasm and ending with a person or persons unknown "drowneded in the Lubagh." Between what he imagines and what I fail to understand, I cannot say I am much the wiser about these ruins. In the next life we will probably be surprised to see how much historical knowledge was more or less like this. He could not, in fact, have picked an easier target for his imagination: all documents relating to events prior to 1650 are lost. The archives were taken to Bordeaux by the exiled brethren in 1652, and transferred to Louvain in 1655; in the confusion of the Napoleonic wars they were lost forever.

"This is the jail yard," says my guide as he darts through a doorway on the left. When I follow him my heart misses a beat: we are in a cloister garth of perfect proportions. Or rather we are in the outline of a cloister, for much of the stonework has been removed, though a few arches have been reconstructed. Despite the devastation, there is a sense of presence and interiority; it is still a place in which to walk and meditate. I feel sufficiently guided now and I try to pay off my young guide, but it is not so easily done: I have been a good listener and he likes me. I have to raise the fee to fifty pence before he agrees to finish. He will make a good business-man; he has already learned, at the age of seven, that you can either be good at a job or so bad that people will pay you to give it up. Or it could be that he just loves his work.

34

It is a blessed gift to be alone here. With a sense of awe I walk the cloister as so many of my forgotten brethren did from the thir-teenth century to the time of its dissolution in the sixteenth, and later when they returned in the seventeenth century. The loss of the archives is an additional tragedy, leaving the priory in a still deeper silence. There are only scraps of information: the brethren came here in 1291 and bought this piece of land from John Bluet, one of the burgesses of the town; a provincial chapter was held here in 1340; the tower and the south transept were added in the fifteenth century. In 1541 the suppressed priory was taken over by "sundry jurors, true and lawful men," along with its cloister and other buildings for the sum of six shillings and eight pence. Writing in exile in 1706, Fr John O'Heyne called this priory *speciosus*, "beautiful", and spoke of its "magnificence". But more important, he said, was the sanctity and learning of the brethren who lived here: *abundavit filiis religione, moribus ac scientia insignibus.* James O'Hurley, a man of great sanctity and learning, was prior here many times, and later became provincial; still later he was Bishop of Emly. Another who followed an almost identical course was Terence Albert O'Brien, twice prior of the neighbouring community at Limerick, also elected provincial; he must have visited here many times. Years later as Bishop of Emly he was hanged in Limerick by Oliver Cromwell's son-in-law, Ireton. At his condemnation, wrote Fr Dominic O'Daly, he foretold Ireton's imminent death. "He told the Tyrant that in a very short time he would be called to give an account of himself before the Tribunal of God." Ireton died soon afterwards, in fact, greatly troubled. "Would that I had never seen that papist bishop," he said, "even from a distance."

"I cannot praise a fugitive and cloistered virtue that never sallies out and sees her adversary," wrote John Milton. Her adversary, however, came to visit her — in the person of Milton's friend and fellow-Puritan, Oliver Cromwell and his blood-frenzied soldiers. What if all the history of this priory were known? It might be a weight too heavy to bear. Perhaps it is a mercy in some ways not to know too much about the sufferings of the past. Krishnamurti says that the first thing needed for a spiritual life is a poor memory. In any case there is no choice in the matter now: the archives are lost and there are centuries of silence.

For me, the silence will be measured in weeks. It will be a

deeper silence than the silence of mountains and the sea; it will be human silence — silent voices. The empty shells of their conversations are everywhere: this corner, these stairs, this doorway heard and saw so much. Those conversations cannot be heard, however, nor even their bearing guessed. The archives are silent; there is nothing left to listen with but the heart.

35

Cloisters have always affected me, and I love to 'collect' them by photographing them. Irish cloisters tended to have a tree at the centre, while the cloisters of continental Europe preferred a well. A four-sided covered walk with a tree or a well at the centre seems to me a perfect image of the inner life. They built from the inside out in those days.

It is probable that a tree stood at the centre of this cloister garth. I imagine its branches solidly there, and its roots burrowing powerfully into the earth. It is a symbol of many things: today, unlike mediaevals, one probably sees it first as a symbol of the self. There is the part above the ground: visible, noisy, restless — the outer self, the personality. And there is the inner self, like the roots of the tree, hidden, silent and still. If I send my imagination down into that underground world I find it terrifying at first: it is a world of total darkness and silence, and nothing moves there — or rather the only movement is growth. Those grotesque shapes are dreadful, but only because we are not used to looking so deeply into the source. I have to expect that the deepest things are dreadful, but not hateful. And I have to expect that they will never be as clear as day. A tree protects its mystery well; no one has ever seen all the roots of a full-grown tree. If a storm blows the tree down, most of the roots remain in the ground, holding its mystery even after death.

Mediaeval people thought first of the tree of life, probably, or the cross of Christ when they saw a tree. The brethren who walked this cloister or looked through a window at this tree would remember the Book of Daniel:

> I saw a tree
> in the middle of the world …

Or perhaps they thought of the Axle-Tree, an image from the later mediaeval period: the stars and planets were thought of as whirling around the Axle-Tree of Heaven, the pivot of the universe. This image was applied to the cross of Christ. A tree was many things: a warning, a sign of hope, a reminder of the Lord's passion and his victory over sin and death. So many of our feelings look pale and petty beside theirs; their exegesis would discover little nourishment in Kilmer's tree "that may in Summer wear a nest of robins in her hair."

Antoninus of Piacenza would probably find here some twigs from a tree planted in the seventh century by St Mocheallog, who gave his name to the town of Kilmallock. It would have to be a direct descendant, of course, of Nathaniel's tree, for that too was a meditation tree, a place of shade in which the man (like Antoninus himself) "in whom there was no guile" was praying when he was seen by the Lord.... And why not? Connections made by the heart are surely just as real as nests of robins.

I have been hovering here for more than an hour, in no hurry to see the rest of the priory; cloisters, after all, were made for hovering. I feel at one with those long-dead brethren who likewise hovered here — hovered around that tree, symbol of life and death.

36

The choir stands silent and empty like a lonely cornfield whose harvest is over. Night has fallen, and when I look up I see the stars of heaven. *Ad te clamamus exules filii Hevae.* Night makes me think of other worlds, other stars; we are creatures of distance. I think of the uncertain lives of my brothers who prayed here in the night. *Ad te suspiramus, gementes et flentes.* Two of them, a young student and a lay brother, were slain by the sword before the high altar, white-robed acolytes leading the solemn procession of death. *In hac lacrymarum valle.* The warm heart of faith pierced by the cold aggression of the sword. *O clemens, o pia, o dulcis Virgo Maria!*

There is nothing left in this choir but the walls pierced by lancet windows. I stand here in the darkness to let it make its presence felt. It is a smaller area than the nave of the church and divided from it by the tower. At the eastern end is a pure Gothic window of five narrow lancets above the place of the high altar. I see its shape darkly; how it must give a sense of grandeur in the early morning! Despite the lack of a roof, the choir retains a sense of intimacy; it is a pleasing shape. Nothing remains but shape, time has taken everything else away. Yet it is enough, it is the essence.

John Ruskin, the nineteenth-century oracle on architectural and other matters, considered decoration the essence: "It gradually became manifest to me," he wrote in *The Seven Lamps of Architecture*, "that the sculpture and painting were in fact the all and all ... that these, which I had long been in the careless habit of thinking subordinate to the architecture, were in fact the entire masters of the architecture; and that the architect who was not a sculptor or a painter was nothing better than a frame-maker on a large scale." He drew the decent conclusion: "I saw that the idea of an independent architectural profession was a mere modern fallacy." He saw architecture as a decorative art merely, and he made a list of suitable decorative themes for churches: "bishops, deans, canons and choristers, birds and flowers." It seems incredible that anyone should have been so insensitive to space. He would dismiss these glorious ruins with the word *frame*! Leaving aside the tracery on the south window of the transept and a few other details, there is no decoration left here; yet how powerful some of these spaces are in their barrenness!

An undecorated space is not nothing; on the contrary, it is all the more clearly seen for the lack of decoration. Walking now in this empty space I begin to reflect on inner spaces, the inner life. Johann Tauler, Eckhart's friend and disciple, said that we must welcome emptiness and find God in it. "We must go into our house, our souls; and all our senses, everything to do with them, and everything which comes to us through them must all be left outside: all images, all forms, everything which our imagination has ever brought us, however rational it may be. Even our reason and its workings must be left outside." It is a kind of knowing that is unknowing; it is emptiness, or the Nothingness that can look at Christians. Like this empty choir it has no decoration at all.

What would Ruskin think of inner spaces, spiritual emptiness? Just as little, probably, as he did of outer spaces. Architecture was about unnecessary features, he said: "If to the stone facing of a bastion be added an unnecessary feature, as a cable mould, that is Architecture." Spirituality then, I suppose, would also consist of decorations and "unnecessary features." We have more in common now, I think, with Tauler's fourteenth century than with Ruskin's nineteenth.

God seems to enjoy destroying our decorations, according to Tauler. "When we go into our house and look for God there, God in his turn looks for us and ransacks the house. He behaves just as we do when we are searching for something, throwing aside one thing after another until we find what we are looking for. This is just what he does to us....And when I say that God seeks us in our house and ransacks it, I mean that in this house, in the depths of our souls, we are utterly deprived of all the ideas and conceptions of God by which we have ever thought of him before. Our house is ransacked; it is as if we had never known anything about God at all. As he seeks for us, this happens again and again; every idea that we ever had of him, every manifestation of him that we have ever known, every conception and revelation of him which we ever had will be taken away from us as he searches to find us."

As I return to the tent I am aware that I have found in these ruins
an even better place than Dunquin in which to think about God and
to pray, to think about immensity and nothingness and the mystery
of time and place. The stars are too vast; when you look at them
without context you are *dislocated*. You should always look at the
stars through something, out of something, *from some place*, or
with some question or interest. Otherwise they will only fill you
with terror. God's immensity, likewise, is overwhelming in the
abstract. You should look consciously at him from some location,
some inner or outer place. In the Christian vision, the dewdrop
does not "slip into the shining sea"; our reality is not absorbed by
God. We stand, a little like these ruins, in irreducible personhood,
but open to God's infinite spaces.

37

*Tu in nobis es, Domine, et nomen sanctum tuum invocatum est
super nos.* The words of Compline, the last Office of the day, keep
returning to the mind: "You, O Lord, are in the midst of us, and we
are called by your name. Do not desert us, O Lord our God...."
Lying in my tent I imagine those words echoing through the
ancient priory. They return to me in Latin, the very stuff of holy
memory. I am grateful that I am old enough to have had Latin in
common with those early Dominicans; it gives a sense of partner-
ship with them.

Painting scenes from the life of Christ on the walls of his
brethren's cells in San Marco, Fra Angelico included a Dominican
in each fresco — though there were no Dominicans in existence
for twelve hundred years after the time of Christ. He understood
a profound truth: when we pray we are all contemporaries. Mythic
time could be called "heart-time". The heart has its own timing, of
which reason knows nothing at all. Heart-time loops to include us

all in one moment of eternity. Prayer once prayed remains for all
time and eternity in the heart of Christ and is being offered forever
to the Father. No one knows anything about the Dominicans who
lived here in the 1430s and 40s while Fra Angelico was painting
those frescoes in Florence; no one knows anything except that they
prayed and preached. Their prayer lives forever; I am their
contemporary, and lying here in the night I pray the psalms of the
Office with them.

> *Domine, refugium factus es nobis*
> *a generatione in generationem* ...

> O Lord, you have been our refuge
> from one generation to the next ...

> Before the mountains were born
> or the earth or the world brought forth,
> you are God, without beginning or end.
> You turn men back into dust
> and say: 'Go back, sons of men.'

> To your eyes a thousand years
> are like yesterday, come and gone,
> no more than a watch in the night.

38

A tall grey man comes intently towards me in the cloister garth and
shakes my hand firmly as if he had known me all his life. His
handshake is cold and hard. He deplores at length the morning's
weather and then speaks of recent weather in general, picking out
flaws that had escaped my notice. But he excuses it on the grounds
that God hides a purpose even in the foulest events. As I wait
patiently to be released again to solitude and prayer his argument
progresses by itself, ranging fluently over all contemporary evils,

but always in the end exhibiting God's wisdom. After half an hour the torrent shows no sign of abating, and I wish I were alone.

But wait! I have only half the picture: his image of the world seems very godly, yes, but there are hidden cankers everywhere. He broods on evil, and his God is a capricious Dad whose ways have to be explained to the neighbours lest they get the wrong impression. Evil is uppermost, or rather innermost. Goodness is remote and improbable, and this is why he has to prove that it exists somewhere. And what more appropriate place than in God? Yet, clearly, it is not safe even there. God has to be defended. This man has taken on himself the responsibility of God's point of view. But his vindication of God arises out of his own need, because I have given no sign that I have any quarrel with the weather or with any of the other problems he mentioned.

I will pray that he gets a better opinion of the world, I tell him, and I begin to take my leave, because I want to return to the tent. But he walks beside me, and soon I see that he has no destination of his own. He is in flight from his own interiority and he intends to invade mine.

I want to protect my secret space from him, and I give the tent a wide berth, like a mother bird protecting her family from a predator. By now he is reaching crescendos in several different keys: his world is filled with traitors and conspirators on the one side and self-defeating softies on the other. Simplified by a cartoonist his philosophy would approach the demi-language of the *Dandy* and the *Beano*: Wham! Pow! Eek!

I have never been so certain of being useless to someone. He is not to be helped. Not now, at any rate. I am sure of it. He is asking no questions, leaving no spaces. There is no silence in his spirit. And he has prescriptions for the whole world. I try to speak of humility. I intend it for him, but he directs it outwards: others should be more humble. His presence begins to chill me to the bone. It is the compacted sediment of great ambitions, wretched failures and fierce angers. It is frustrated omnipotence.

I have made a resolution to spend an hour or so in the parish church every day, and I decide to head for there now. This much silence is sure to shake him off, and I will be allowing the church to serve one of its ancient purposes — sanctuary from the enemy.

Free of his entanglements I breathe freely for several minutes, and it has the freshness of a new discovery. That great echoing space welcomes like a mother and it cares nothing for imagined conflicts or twisted emotions. The Lord is there who understands the secrets of hearts. I pray long for my neurotic friend in flight from his interiority. Gradually it becomes clear that I am not praying simply for one man; I am praying for myself too, and for the whole human race heavy with inner life. He is part of what I am; he is the perfect counterpoint of what I am trying to attain; he is my brother. What a burden the inner life can become! It will weigh us to the ground if we see ourselves only as individual unfortunates. Who will roll away the heavy stone so that we can rise with Christ? Who indeed? An angel — a messenger of God — or God himself?

Can we ever heal one another's interiority? I believe that the Lord alone can do so — and those who are so close to the Lord that God himself might mistake them.

I imagine the inner world like a city: not a grand city but an impenetrable complex of hovels half-built or falling down — projects begun with joy but never completed, or beautiful things neglected and abandoned. There is no main street because fifty streets are called the main street, a different one each day. Whole neighbourhoods seethe with violence; others are haunted by indefinable fears. Briars and nettles and every kind of under-growth block the entrances and windows of houses. Yet here and there you can see beautiful, unselfconscious things: a peaceful window, a corner where one might live. All in all it is a jungle. If you are not going far you will be all right, but to enter deeply there without a guide is to be lost. The Lord alone can guide you through the deepest places, pointing out good things that give you heart, steering you clear of others, choosing the right time to take you through certain areas, moving always in the right direction.

   As I leave the church I am sustained by this image of the Lord
as guide in the inner city; and I make my way along the street and
down towards the corner of the meadow where my tent is pitched.
   To my horror, there he is! — investigating, sniffing, walking
around the tent, strumming guy-ropes to test their tension, standing back to think, consumed with empty curiosity. "Are you
camping?" he asks superfluously as I come up. "Yes," I answer
simply, as I open the flaps, crawl inside and draw the zips together
after me. He attempts to continue the conversation but I remain
enclosed in grand silence. Interiority can make a temple out of thin
sheets of nylon. I will try to be his silence. I am closer to him in
reality than if I had consented to another of his bouts of recrimin-
ation. I will be his temple. Or rather I will try to be my own, and
he may remember his. He attempts to knock on the nylon flaps but
that is a task not easily accomplished. They are stouter in that
respect than doors of oak. For the first time I am comfortable with
my curious friend. Some kind of truth is expressed perfectly in this
arrangement; and sooner or later the truth will set us free. I love it
when things are reduced to such simple essences. I am comfortable here. Porcupines, snails and tortoises do something like this.
I should honour them more! All honour to every centre of being
in the whole creation! All praise to the Lord who contains us in all
our confusion!

39

For there he keeps me safe in his tent
in the day of evil.
He hides me in the shelter of his tent.

There is one thing I ask of the Lord,
for this I long,

> to live in the house of the Lord
> all the days of my life,
> to savour the sweetness of the Lord,
> to behold his temple.

Yes, he hid me in the shelter of his tent. After half an hour I emerged to find that my tormentor had vanished, and I made my way back to the ruins. I am sitting now in a corner of the empty choir; it is midday and I am alone. It takes a while to accept again the utter emptiness of this space; I have found that the imagination first diminishes and then fills remembered spaces. Nothingness is hard to remember.

As there is empty space here, there is also empty time: time to look around me, "to behold his temple." Tent and temple, it suddenly occurs to me, were both places of God's presence.

The patriarchs and the early Israelites were tent-dwelling nomadic shepherds; not till they settled in Canaan did they begin to live in houses. Their God lived among them — in a tent. "Build me a sanctuary," he said to Moses, "so that I may live among them." A midrashic legend tells of the surprise that Moses felt on hearing this. "Surely the Divine Presence fills the heavens and the earth; am I to encompass it within the confines of a tent?" The Holy One replied, "Erect for me a tent, twenty boards to the north, twenty boards to the south, and eight boards to the west, and I will descend and confine my presence within their bounds." The instructions from God were so detailed that it could easily be reconstructed today. The builder-in-chief was Bezalel, a name that means "in the shadow of God".

The Tent (or Tabernacle, which is from the Latin word for *tent*) was divided — by a veil of magnificent tapestry — into the sanctuary, which was thirty feet long and fifteen wide, and the Holy of Holies, which was fifteen feet square. The Holy of Holies was in fact a perfect cube lined with gold, symbolising perfection, permanence and eternity. The only object in that pitch-dark space was the Ark of the Testimony, which was a chest of acacia wood plated inside and out with pure gold and containing the Testimony, that is, the tablets on which the Ten Commandments were written. This was the holiest place on earth, the place of God's Presence.

Later, when the Israelites settled and built a permanent Temple in Jerusalem, called Solomon's Temple, it had the same structure as the Tent but it was of course on a grander scale. As before, a curtain closed off access to the Holy of Holies, now a cube of thirty feet on each side. The Letter to the Hebrews tells that "it is entered only once a year, and then only by the High Priest who must go in by himself and take the blood to offer for his own faults and the people's." Solomon's Temple was destroyed in 587 B.C. and replaced by the Temple of Zerubbabel, which in turn was replaced by the Temple of Herod, designed on a vast scale and begun in 19 B.C. This last Temple is the one that Jesus knew. In his time, however, the Ark that used to lie there was missing; the Holy of Holies was an empty space.

St John's Gospel reports that Jesus identified the Temple with his own body. "Destroy this temple," he said to the Jews, "and in three days I will raise it up." They replied, "it has taken forty-six years to build this temple, and will you raise it up in three days?" "But he spoke of the temple of his body," John adds. At the moment that Jesus died on the cross there were strange occurrences: "there was darkness over the whole land while the sun's light failed" and in the Temple the curtain barring access to the Holy of Holies was suddenly "torn in two from top to bottom."

The Holy of Holies was laid open by his death: it is perhaps the most powerful symbol in all of literature. The Christian tradition interprets it in several ways: through Jesus, the new High Priest, the holiness of God is made accessible to all; no longer is God hidden, he is made visible in Jesus; the old high priests offered the blood of goats and calves for their own sins and those of the people, but Jesus offers his own blood; the Jerusalem Temple and its cult is abolished and Jesus is the new Temple. St Paul extends the range of this symbol to include all disciples of Jesus: all Christians are temples of the living God: "the temple of the living

God is what we are."

This ancient choir where I now sit is empty, like the Holy of Holies. The Holy One whom the whole earth and the heavens cannot contain is present here, but 'here' is now wherever Jesus is. Jesus is the Place where God is accessible to us.

Where, I ask, does this leave my huts and houses, my corners and cottages and cloisters? I really have no answer to that at present; I will have to leave it for the unconscious mind to turn over in its sleep.

40

"As for what they say about Lot's wife, that she is diminished in size by being licked by animals, it is not true; she stands in exactly the same condition as she originally was." If we did not know him so well we would have taken Antoninus for a comedian; but he did not have sufficient distance from his experience to be a comedian. This afternoon I met a man who had such a playful relationship with reality that he was able to tell tales as tall as Antoninus's. Comedy is perhaps the opposite of naivety, and like all opposites they have something in common.

I first saw him in a hardware store where I had gone to buy oil for my lantern. Business was slow, or rather stopped, and he was telling the owner a story about a dog he owned long ago, a dog of exceptional beauty. I pretended an interest in farm implements, emulsion paints, and balls of bailer twine. This animal had a wonderful coat which everyone admired, and he had a good attitude to all living things, with the one exception of other dogs: he seemed to think the world would be a better place without them. He died eventually, of course, and was missed by his human friends. The next day a neighbour made a good suggestion.

"Tadhg, why don't you get the dog's hide tanned?"

"What good would that do?"

"Well, you could still admire the coat then, and maybe the tailor could turn it into something useful for you, like a waistcoat."

It was done, and it was the finest waistcoat in Kilmallock. There was only one problem: whenever he passed Murphy's house and their dogs ran out barking, the hair on the waistcoat would stand up on end and become very uncomfortable.

When I laughed behind a barricade of paint-tins his face appeared in an opening between the tins and his smile filled the whole gap. "It's no word of a lie," he said. "It's God's truth," he repeated as he came around the shelving to shake my hand. Another customer arrived and I had the storyteller all to myself.

"Did that dog ever have pups?" I asked as we left the shop. I was planning a little joke about waistcoats for the boys.

"No, he had not. Not with his attitude. Couldn't stand sight nor sound of another dog, nor a bitch but as little." This man, I realised, takes his stories seriously; he does not classify them readily as fiction and put them aside.

"Talking about hides," he continues, "I had a horse twenty years ago ... " and he launches into another story as we walk together along the street. He comes to a sudden halt just in front of a busy grocery shop in order to concentrate on the story. As we stand among the shoppers I have a vague feeling that there are different time-levels here, and that I have no idea which of them, if any, is real. This mixing of time-dimensions is found continually in Ireland, and that German historian of the last century, who thought to write "absolute history", describing the past "as it really was, *wie es eigentlich gewesen*," would be at a sore loss here. This horse I am to hear about, is it the grey horse of history? Who knows? It is a horse, I think, of every colour.

"He was the finest horse in the parish." I missed some of the early part of the story through inattention; few people belong more to the present than shoppers, and I am not sure if I am to situate myself among them in the present, or on some other level. It seems that Tadhg was taking a cartload of porter to a publican when he stopped to talk to a neighbour. As they talked, the horse began to drink unnoticed from one of the barrels; he soon got a colic and appeared to be as dead as a stone. There was nothing for it but to take him to the knackers and try to get a fair price for the skin. He got twenty-five shillings. That night his wife woke him up with a jab of her elbow. "The horse is in the yard," she said. He could hardly be blamed for not believing this straight away, but when he was persuaded to look out he saw that the horse was really there, with no skin on him. He went out and stabled him for the night, and next morning he went straight to the knackers to get the skin back. It had just been sent off in the lorry with other skins, they told him. He asked if they had any skins of any sort left. They had nothing but three or four sheepskins, and he brought them with him. He placed them around the horse and began to stitch them together with wire, but soon he ran out of wire and had to use some brambles that were growing nearby. "And as sure as I'm standing here,I got three good cuts of wool off that horse every year; and I would have got four if it wasn't for the children pulling it off as they climbed up to pick the blackberries."

"These are wonderful stories," I tell him.

"And every one of them truer than the last," he assures me.

That much could be true at any rate, I think.

"We used to swap many a story long ago before the television came in. At the end of a night you couldn't remember who told which story, so maybe some of my stories are Pa Doherty, God rest him's."

That is how traditions are made in every part of the world: in ancient Greece, on the Great Blasket and in Kilmallock itself.

We are walking now along the main street, and he enquires about myself: where I come from and where I am going. He knows Beeing well, a fact that surprises me as usual. When he was a young man he once had to take a greyhound to someone who lived there — a distance of about forty miles. He missed his lift, so they set out running, he and the greyhound; the exercise would do them both good. They made it in two hours; and they would have made it in an hour-and-a-half if the greyhound hadn't got tired near Buttevant.... He has a story for every person, place and thing. He asks what brings me to Kilmallock, and when I tell him (somewhat apologetically) what I am doing and why I needed three months' rest, he sums up my situation with exquisite wisdom and kindness: it is no delay, he says, to stop and edge the tool.

He has to leave me now, for his wife is waiting for him: a great girl, he says, the best in Ireland. Once he was ploughing a few acres near the house when she came out and sat down to watch.

"Tadhg," she said after a while, "you're working far too hard; you're killing yourself. And look: there's a hole in your sock, and your heel will be getting sore. Here, go and have a drink for yourself."

He had about a half-acre of ploughing left to do, and he spent no more than half-an-hour in the pub; but when he returned he found that she had finished the ploughing, and wasn't she turning the heel of the second sock!

"Where is she waiting?" I ask. I see nothing ahead but the empty street.

Pain clouds his face. He moves a step closer to me and lowers his head; it is like a confession:

"She's buried beyond in the graveyard these thirty years."

41

"When you visualised a man or a woman carefully," wrote Graham Greene, "when you saw the lines at the corners of the eyes, the shape of the mouth, how the hair grew, it was impossible to hate. Hate was just a failure of imagination." In that passage Graham Greene does not mean by 'imagination' a facility for seeing what is not there ('fantasy' would be a better word for that); on the contrary, he means a facility for seeing what *is* there. If it is true, as he says, that hate is a failure of this kind of imagination, then love requires the presence and the use of it.

Night is falling, and I am thinking with an ache in my heart about my storytelling friend. He has every kind of imagination: most vividly, the ability to see what is not there; but he also sees and expresses touchingly what is. I could never imagine him in flight from reality; he is too rugged, too earthy, for that. He possesses, in addition to fantasy, the kind of imagination that makes great love possible. The pain of loss has not been denied, and so it has not festered in his heart. As for his stories, I hardly think that "God's truth", which he invokes so often, could be narrower than our most fertile imagination. *Wie es eigentlich gewesen*! Such an historian would have recorded the date of Tadhg's wife's death and called that the 'absolute' truth of the matter! How pretentious and crude to think that human events have no 'density', no depth, no labyrinths: that they are two-dimensional like a page of print! Severed from Tadhg's loving imagination, what is left of her death? Can there ever be truth without love? Yes, but it is always either trivial or destructive. Lucifer was an Angel of Light; then his imagination failed him, he learned to hate and became the Prince of Darkness; but the name of the First Truth remains eternally Love.

It is a reality I have not thought much about on this pilgrimage: love. That one meeting with my storyteller may have much to teach me. It is clear that he has gone ahead and looked into the Void, and he has returned with love — and wonderful stories.

42

There is a full moon tonight, and I am sitting at the mouth of the tent watching it with its reflection in the Lubagh. What an irony that such a barren body should have anything to do with fertility!

Yet it seems to insist on its femininity in most languages that divide nouns by gender. And how can such a dead thing cause madness in the living? It works, perhaps, by opposite effect: it looks so cold and reasonable that it drives people the other way!

"There are three kinds of men who do not understand women," runs an Irish saying, a *seanfhocal*, "young men, middle-aged men and old men!" Not understanding them, we make caricatures: 'feminine psychology', 'feminine images'; and women, being wiser, only play with them; they love to try them on and change them like clothes! Like clothes, they are only rough approximations of the human reality. They are quite abstract (like caricatures); they even have the appearance of philosophical principles at times: the Eternal-Feminine, *das Ewigweibliche*.

I think back tonight on my houses and huts and hermitages, and on the forceful way that they make their presence felt. I heard a psychologist declare that the house is a 'feminine image'; it reminds one of the womb and the woman's instinct to enfold and nourish children; and so it becomes an image of intimacy. But I think that by calling the house a 'feminine image', men are implying (despite the distinctions they sometimes make) that intimacy is the concern of women only. 'Intimacy' means depth, and that is surely everyone's concern. The simple equation of house with femininity is a spent cliché. It marks the place where one has stopped thinking; it pinpoints nothing, explains nothing and leads nowhere. 'Masculine' and 'feminine' in our world are the problem, not the answer. Goethe called man and woman "God's two most beautiful ideas", and he then went on about the Eternal-Feminine. I would prefer to think we were one idea, with a wonderful variation on the theme, rather than two ideas. It is dangerous for men and women to weave dreamy myths about one another; they only serve to obscure our common humanity, and they often restrict to one side what really belongs to both.

"A woman and a man are unlike, but in love they are alike," says Eckhart. He does not mean that their loving is alike, but that they are made alike when they love. Perhaps it is because they enter their full humanity only when they learn to love. Eckhart mentions the love of men and women in order to say that our love of God makes us like God. "Scripture rightly says that God took woman from the man's rib and side and not from the head or from the feet.... He did not make her from the head or the feet, so that she would be neither woman nor man to him, but so that she should be his peer." We are God's peers when we love God; God and we are unlike, but in love we are made alike.

I think of Tadhg's love for his long-lost wife. He has shown me, as far as anyone can, what God is like. "I have loved you with an everlasting love." Today, thirty years after her death, deeper than death, it touched my heart.

43

It is raining heavily and I am sheltering in the cloister — in the one part of it that is able to offer shelter. This is a good time of year to be here, better than summer. Very fine weather is somehow a little too expansive; it makes light of loss, discouraging memory. But this October morning's rain gives a sense of interiority, reducing the space in which one can move. It is delightful to be protected by this building: I had been regarding it as a frail creature in need of protection itself. Now, for a short space, it has a little of its earlier strength, like an aged father who has one day so free of sickness that we are reminded of what he was.

One side of the cloister-walk is covered, and I am able to pace back and forth along its sixty-foot length, looking out at the emptiness of the rest and imagining how it must have been. A paradoxical fact about emptiness is that there is not enough room in it for vanity or possessiveness or any of the other works of the ego. There is an utter humility about these stones and these empty spaces; they pretend to nothing and they ask for nothing; they tell a sacred truth and then fall silent, accentuating nothing. The sacred truth for which this space was measured out was God; it was a space for prayer and meditation; not vanity but love was its meaning.

Tadhg and his wife are still with me as I walk here. They had more than the normal measure of loss and emptiness. But, as I think about them, I begin to see that love needs emptiness and poverty of spirit — in some measure. Lovers throw nets of poetry and romance to trap one another, and from the moment they are caught in one another's ego, there is only suffering. They never intended to love, but only to possess and enslave. In the myth, Eros makes a paradise for Psyche, but he makes her promise one thing: that she will not look at him and will not enquire into any of his ways. He wants to possess her without relating to her. The lust for possession and power are mistaken for love, and they have many clever ways of disguising themselves under its appearances. If this is so in human love, it is even more likely to be so in one's love of God. Because love of God is our highest realisation, it is the point where we are most likely to nourish all our subtlest vanities and illusions. That is why we have to begin by looking into emptiness. Then we continue as we began: in emptiness. "Stand still," said Eckhart, "and do not waver from your emptiness."

The Emptiness, the Nothingness, that looks at a Christian is not Stoic apathy or Taoist calm; it is simply the space needed for loving. St John of the Cross engraved these words at the beginning of *The Ascent of Mount Carmel*: "Nothing, nothing, nothing, nothing, nothing, nothing, and even on the Mount nothing." "The soul must stand," he said, "in the centre of its humility." The mind is capable of looking into this Nothingness briefly, to its horror, but only the heart can consent to live in it. St Thérèse of Lisieux studied in the school of her fellow-Carmelite St John of the Cross and looked into the eye of Nothingness; yet she was above all things loving and joyful. Perhaps only those who live like this can really know what love and joy mean.

My storytelling friend, I tell myself, hardly guesses that he has put me on the track of love, reminding me of things spoken by the saints. But perhaps I am not doing him justice: his vivid imagination would encompass this and more. Imagination, like love, "believes all things, hopes all things, endures all things."

44

"The striking thing about love and will in our day," wrote Rollo May, "is that, whereas in the past they were always held up to us as the answer to life's predicaments, they have now themselves become the problem." The problem appears to be different in the two cases: we hear constantly of love, and we seldom hear of will. Yet Rollo May is surely right in placing the two together. The love we hear so much about is often a cloak for a far different reality. Perhaps real love is as rare as will. St Thomas Aquinas identified love as an act of will; to love, he said, is to will good to another: *bonum velle alicui*. That is something to meditate on today.

I found a rough wooden box here in the cloister, and it is a useful seat. It may be that there was a bench in this very place in the ancient days and that this was someone's favourite place for thinking and praying on a wet day.

It was the sole prescription for too long: will and will-power; the reaction was bound to come. There had been too much incompetence, in the manner of a handyman who used the same tool — a hammer — for every job. The only adjectives we used to describe the will were *strong* and *weak*. That was a sure sign that something was wrong: strong and weak could describe a brute animal just as well. Persons who were noted for their will-power reminded me of a rhinoceros: one or two points up at the front, and a ton of brute force to back them up. There came a reaction of course: not will-power now but "a meaningful experience" was the answer, or feelings or value-clarification or some form of

therapy. Now, the handyman had every kind of tool in his bag —
except a hammer. He was in fact as restricted as before. There must
be a balanced way; there must be ways to reclaim the will, and to
civilize it.

A hammer? It is not a good metaphor, but not as bad as it seems.
A hammer is a precision instrument, though it does not look it. Try
using one and you will see! There has to be the right amount of
energy in the right place at the right time. The will, too, is for
precise use: sensitive measurement of energy, perfect accuracy
and timing. Our list of adjectives might expand from two to three;
we might speak of *skilful* use of the will. And why stop there?
Describe it to us with the fervour of a lover! Let it be *gentle*, for
gentleness is part of real strength. Let it be *faithful* and *attentive*
and *persevering*. In short, let it be *human* and *loving*.

Love without will is only sentimentality; love with the wrong
kind of will is brutal. I am only as civilized as my will. And my
attitude to God is also shaped by this: if I am sentimental or brutal,
my God will appear in the same light. How can I say sensible
things about the will of God if I am saying absurd things about
human will?

I remember Dunquin and Psalm 118; *precepts, statutes, decrees* took on a meaning that was not merely external and judicial.
Now, *will* can join the ranks of redeemed words in my mind.

> Long have I known that your will
> is established for ever ...
> Bend my heart to your will
> and not to love of gain.
> The justice of your will is eternal;
> if you teach me I shall live.

The will has often been associated with external force and
control; but it is possibly our most intimate faculty; it is what
makes love to be love rather than a tangle of neuroses.

As I leave my wooden box where I have been sitting for an hour,
it occurs to me that all the arguments (or at least those I can

remember) against the freedom of the will are founded on a great fear, deeper than the fear of death: the fear to love. In England in the 1870s a famous experiment with a frog caused a great stir in scientific circles. Its brain was removed, yet the frog could still perform some apparently purposeful actions. This proved to the wise men of the time that there was no longer any need to hold a spiritual view of human beings, since physiology now explained everything. One of them wrote gleefully that "a frog with no brain has destroyed more theology than all the doctors of the Church with their whole brains could ever build up again." I consider now that it comes back to whether you want to live like a brainless frog or like a doctor of the Church.

45

I thought of the days of long ago
and remembered the years long past.
At night I mused within my heart;
I pondered and my spirit questioned.
Has his love vanished forever?
Has his promise come to an end?

I have finished the Office of Evening Prayer and I am sitting in the empty choir. There is a wonderful peace all around; clues to our immortality lie scattered everywhere. God is in this holy place. "How lovely is your dwelling place, Lord, God of Hosts.... " Suddenly a sound, high up, catches my attention, and when I look up I see to my alarm that my young guide has reappeared. It is not his presence so much as his position, thirty feet above the ground, that causes my heart to jump. Holding on to the wall with one hand he waves expansively to me, like a gargoyle set free from stone, and shouts something unintelligible. "Come down, slowly!" I shout back. In response he climbs even higher over the east window of the choir. I try to quantify the danger: would a promise of fifty pence bring him down too fast? I realise, just in time, that while it might indeed bring him down, it would also send him up many more times. "Stay there!" I shout up at him and I leave in a leisurely manner through the side door of the choir.

Five minutes later I meet him in the cloister. "It's a very dangerous thing to climb up there!" I tell him.

"My Dad used to spend most of his time on the walls when he was young. It was the only place my Granny couldn't catch him."

I understand his speech better now; one of us must have improved. So, climbing the priory walls is a family tradition; I need not have worried. And the priory's life is a wider reality than I allowed. I suppose it has never ceased to support some form of life throughout the centuries; and its life has still not ended. This small boy's way of seeing it is quite different from mine: to me it is an ancient priory, to him it is a playground. It is whatever you take it to be.

"Did you say this was a castle?" I ask him.

"No, a church."

"I think you said a few weeks ago that it was a castle; what made it change into a church?"

"I saw you saying your prayers in it when I was up on the walls."

"And will it still be a church tomorrow?"

"I don't know, maybe a castle or a jail."

You can turn a ruin into anything you like, just as you can a dead person. A dead person's life belongs to you and you can redesign it from start to finish, any way you like. The dead seem so invulnerable; yet in another way they are completely at our mercy. I suppose one's own past offers a similar freedom — which would be a great mercy.

When I begin to pay attention again he is telling a story about his bicycle. He got a puncture once and his grandfather fixed it for him with a postage stamp. Another time, the valve-rubber was worn out, and his grandfather fixed that too; he had no valve-rubber so he used an earthworm instead.

"Is your grandfather's name Tadhg, by any chance?"

"Yeh."

46

It is said of Nijinsky, one of the world's greatest dancers, that some scientists puzzled over his relationship with gravity; they could not understand how one could move like that. He would leap into the air with such grace and when he came down, he seemed to come down slowly, as if the law of gravity had been suspended. He was asked, "How do you do it?" He replied, "I don't know. Except that I love dancing." And later, on reflection, he said, "When you love dancing you don't live under the law of gravity, you live under the law of grace."

I have been reading the first chapter of St John's Gospel. "The law was given through Moses; grace and truth came through Jesus Christ." It was that verse that brought Nijinsky to mind. The light of the lantern shines adequately through the closed flaps of the tent, which keep out the fumes and the cold alike. The tent is tall enough for me to sit on a meditation stool inside it. This last hour before going to sleep is the most peaceful of all. The pyramid shape of the tent, with its peak just over my head, is like a gesture of prayer: all creatures reaching up to God, surpassing earthly gravity.

It is easy to see images of prayer, to find metaphors and stories that speak of it; but in a sense they are all external to it. What is it in itself? No, that is not the right question. There is no 'it'; there is no such thing as prayer. There are people who pray. What do they do? They do countless different things. But is there some essence underlying all the different forms? Is there some quality of spirit or some inner movement without which there would be no prayer?

If there is, it is surely a movement of the will, a leaning towards God, a kind of 'outward' or 'upward' gravitation that happens still 'within' the spirit. (How self-conscious our words become when they try to describe essential things!) I am trying to see clearly *how* one is to "go out," as Tauler put it, "away from the self, above the self." It seems to be a kind of opposite gravitation: away from self-absorption and all lower mergings of the self, and leaning towards the Holy Mystery revealed in Jesus as "grace and truth". All our new adjectives to describe the will can find their full measure here: gentle, skilful, faithful, attentive, persevering.

Mediaeval theologians said that God was the *causa finalis*, the goal, of all creatures; all things seek him by their very nature. Is this not a kind of gravitation? Are we not falling continually ,towards God? Yes, but is gravitation not *passive*? Is there anything you need to *do*? Like other creatures, said the mediaevals, we human beings seek God by our very nature; but our nature is our full nature: it includes our mind and will. "Human beings attain their final end by knowing and loving God," wrote St Thomas Aquinas, *cognoscendo et amando Deum.* There is a tendency in our time to identify our nature with our instincts alone, or with a few spontaneous reactions, or perhaps with the brainless frog in us. So in answer to my question I have to say: this kind of gravitation (I should call it the law of grace) is both active and passive. It is a pull from beyond, but it is a pull on my mind and will as much as on the rest of my nature. I co-operate with it by knowing and loving, *cognoscendo et amando*. God sees my nature whole and is not inclined to bypass my mind and will.

This movement of the will, which is probably the heart of prayer, is a beautiful play of activity and passivity, a balancing of the two in the subtlest ways; it is a kind of trembling at the threshold where the two meet to play. There has been a strong emphasis on the active side, and the imagery of the spiritual journey shows a bias here: we have been forever climbing mountains or ladders of perfection. But why should we not speak also of *falling* towards God? Why not meditate on his attractiveness and allow ourselves to experience it at the playful threshold? The word *attractive* comes from the Latin *trahere*, which means *to pull* (that is also where tractors come from!) We are often advised to let God be God; well, let him be attractive, let him pull us to himself. His pull is stronger than that of gravity; unlike gravity, which only attracts bodies to bodies, he draws the entire person, mind and will included, to himself.

Where I sit in meditation the central pole just behind my back supports the tent, pushing up its pyramid shape with a single thrust. The tent remains a potent symbol of prayer; and the pole (if it were possible to imagine a tent being simultaneously pushed and drawn up) might be a symbol of the human will. I read about an African people who always made the old man's walking-stick from the main beam that supported the house. A main beam and a walking-stick have much in common: they are like the human spine. And I want to add to the list: a tent-pole, and a will that soars up to God.

47

I am drawn back once again to this place of unutterable emptiness, the choir. Unlike the mediaeval Dominican churches of Sligo and Burrishoole, this one has lost its high altar, though the sanctuary area is quite clearly defined. I am sitting opposite the sacristy door, and it is easy to imagine one of the mornings without number when priests came in procession through it to celebrate Mass.

Confitemini Domino quoniam bonus:

Let us bless the Lord for he is good,
for his mercy endures for ever.

Approaching the altar the priest bows deeply and prays: *Aufer a nobis, Domine:* take away our sins, O Lord, that we may be worthy to enter with pure minds into the Holy of Holies, through Christ our Lord. The Holy of Holies is laid open by the death of Christ; his death is re-enacted in all times and places through the Mass. "Mythic time" can now come to earth as "sacramental time". This kind is different from chronological time; it loops in and out of eternity. The Greeks saw *Chronos* as a monster that devoured its offspring; but sacramental time sustains us with the body and blood of Christ.

Credo in unum Deum, Patrem omnipotentem ... The Creed is like architecture; it is the architecture of the faith. It is like entering a cathedral and looking around at the great spaces and the intricate detail. It is the story of what has been and what will be. *Et incarnatus est.* The Word became flesh and dwelt among us. The eternal God has entered the world of time. He has entered our time and not swallowed it up. Nietzsche refused to imagine this possible. "God is a thought that makes all that is straight crooked and all that stands giddy. What? Would time be gone and all that is transitory only a lie?" Yet there it is, the firm faith of the ages. *Sub Pontio Pilato passus* ... He did not suffer in some kind of cyclical time, like a Hindu god, but on a precise and publicly verifiable date in history, "when Pontius Pilate was governor of Judea." Sacramental time is the same kind of mystery as the incarnation itself: the presence of the eternal in our time. Time is not swallowed up, for all that Nietzsche can say, just as the human nature of Jesus was not swallowed up by his divinity. He rose on the third day...and he will come again in glory to judge the living and the dead. "I will see you before the Tribunal of God." The story is not exhausted in human lifetimes; I look for the resurrection of the dead, *et vitam venturi saeculi,* the life of the world to come. Amen! the choir responds. Amen! sing all the generations of brethren who offered Mass at this altar. Their Amen! lives forever in the heart of Christ. Despite the disbelief of Nietzsche, Amen! Despite the cruelty of Cromwell, Amen! Despite the ravages of time, Amen! Amen! Amen!

Memento Domine,omnium circumstantium. Remember, Lord,
all those who are standing about. Someone you love, said Eckhart,
though he or she may be thousands of miles away, is closer than
someone beside you whom you do not love. The choir is empty,
yet it is swarming with invisible presences. At the foot of the altar
kneel the two who died there by the sword, Gerald, a young student
and David a lay-brother; Henry Burgatt, who was once given a gift
of invisibility even in this life: when priest-hunters were searching
for him they could not see him though he was praying in the room
and was plainly visible to all the Catholics present; two priests
who are not only invisible but anonymous, and who did not escape
the priest-hunters; and countless others of different periods. They
are all here present; they are my contemporaries in sacramental
time.

Cromwell's fellow-Puritans wielded another sword, the sword
of derision. Their 'Jack-in-the-Box' was a mockery of the Real
Presence in the tabernacle; the box had "hocus pocus" painted on
the lid, a corruption of the words of consecration, *hoc est corpus.*...
Yet in spite of all that can ever be said or done, "this is my body
which is given for you".

I once saw and held in my hand a chalice that was used on this
altar. Every year the Dominicans of Limerick bring it back here to
its home and use it at a Mass celebrated in the ruins. The long story
of the faith takes up every detail that helps to make its continuity
visible.

"This is the chalice of my blood", flowing through all the
generations, joining their many stories to the Christian story.

"As often as you do these things, you will do them in remembrance of me."

48

You stand under leaves, your feet in shallows,
She eyes you steadily from the beginning of the world.

Ted Hughes, *Low Water*

All rivers are reminders that life is passing, but the curving
Lubagh, like the river in the poem, "a beautiful idle woman," adds
its own comment: it is passing slowly. Having lived here for three
weeks at the most leisurely pace for many years, I know that I can
move now without running; I have a hunch that it is time to move
on.

I will leave tomorrow morning after visiting my friends. Tonight is for looking back.

My huts and hermitages have become more open; they can even
dispense with roofs. They are no longer for protection but for
marking the essence of place. They are empty, without ornament,
willing to be "ransacked" again and again. They are symbols of the
dark place described by Eckhart, the highest part of the soul,
"where no image ever shone in." That is a place of darkness and
emptiness, like the Holy of Holies; and so it is 'natural' for God
to be there. "There is a power in the soul," said Eckhart, "and by
virtue of being like nothing, this power is like God. Just as God is
like nothing, so too this power is like nothing."

Love that does not come from that place is always hiding or
pretending something. That dark place, symbolised by these lean
images, is also the source of real joy.

As I reflect on it, a distinction becomes clear: between happiness and joy. Happiness is always caused; there is always a reason
why one is happy; and when that cause is removed, happiness
vanishes. But joy is uncaused; it comes from the deepest source,
and so it never needs to be bought, it cannot be bought. Happiness
wants to be continuous and the smallest interference can destroy
it, but one spark of joy is enough for weeks or months. It is one

thing the acquisitive world cannot give; it has to be received as a gift. Happiness is enjoyed by cats and dogs, but only we know joy. It is a taste of God's kind of existence.

Time, too, has changed. 'Mythic time' was like a Platonic essence, aspired to but never touching the earth. Sacramental time, however, is incarnated in worldly time: it is mythic time come down to earth. And one should not limit this to the moments when we celebrate the sacraments. All life, for a Christian, has a sacramental quality about it; and so every moment of time is sacramental.

Night brings its grandeur once again, a last time for me in this place. I will visit here in spirit, especially at night, as long as I live; and after that, I may live here forever with my long-lost brothers, in the heart of Christ.

49

Do not say, 'It is morning,' and dismiss it with a name of yesterday. See it for the first time as a new-born child that has no name.

Rabindranath Tagore

The day you leave familiar things behind looks, yes, like a new-born child, even like an orphan. It is hard to leave. I have been finding excuses to delay a little longer: I must sit in the choir one last time, walk around the cloister one last time, look at the windows, walk through my favourite doorway.... To leave here is to experience another of the ransackings that Tauler spoke of. There is only one way to go, and that is to begin to go.

Someone told me about a friend who made a retreat given by a Zen Master. Her friend was a very bookish man who offered explanations of everything, even when they were not sought. On the very first evening the Master asked the retreatants to attempt the lotus posture. A variety of painful efforts was made. When he came to the bookish man he saw that no effort was being made at all. Instead there was an explanation: "I am a western man, and in the west we are not used to these postures. For that reason I am only a beginner, as you can see.... " Without pausing for an instant the Master gave him a painful whack on the back and shouted, "Begin!" It makes perfect sense: if you are a beginner, begin!

Finally I took that Zen Master's advice and loaded the Honda for the road. Rust was beginning to form on the chain, a further omen that it is time to go. I have decided to visit (for a few days only) another mediaeval Dominican ruin, which I have seen in photographs. It lies at the head of Lough Derg on the river Shannon, in the town of Portumna, about sixty miles north of here. My only physical tie with Kilmallock now is the tent. It is spared till last. All the other baggage is loaded, and now comes its fall. The pegs are drawn, the pole removed, the nylon shivers and collapses, and suddenly the tent is no longer a place but only a thing. This moment always troubles me; it is like an annihilation. The place where I lived till a moment ago is nothing now but a patch of flattened grass.

Yes, Brother Tauler, God ransacks our house.

50

The road is not loved for itself. As I travel I realise that I enjoy stopping more than I do travelling. Perhaps the excitement of travelling is the excitement of hope, hope that the future will be better than the present, that it will give us what we lack. No instance of travel ever satisfies the need to travel. It is a lust; once gratified, it demands more. Ariosto expressed this vividly:

Come segue la lepre il cacciatore
Al freddo, al caldo, alla montagna, al lito;
Ne più l'estima poi che presa vede,
Et sol dietro a chi fugge affretta il piede.

(So the hunter follows the hare, in the cold and heat, on the mountain and along the shore. But once he has caught it he cares no more for it; he only chases what flees from him.)

Much of the travelling we do is not travelling at all but hunting. It is only a dissipation and a flight from reality. Yet it is the most common experience of emptiness. "*Stand still*, and do not waver from your emptiness": *that* is the emptiness to look into. The other, the lust for movement, the chase, you can scarcely see into at all, since it is directed blindly outwards to its objects.

I once heard on the radio a conversation between two French novelists. When asked where they would most love to travel, one of them said he would travel, if he could, the whole world, every part of the surface of the globe; the other, more introspective, said he would love to stay on this one spot and sink into the earth, deeper and deeper. If you allow for their expression being a little *exagérée*, these two pointed a profound theme to meditate on.

My own route today is a straight line along the surface: to Limerick city and north along the Shannon. A confrere from this part of the country told us once that his father tackled the pony one day very long ago and drove as far as the Shannon, twelve miles, then home again. He said to his family when he returned, "There's no doubt about it, it's a great experience to travel!" We laughed; but it is possible that that man experienced travel more deeply than many who fly thousands of miles. He was not blinded by a lust for movement, and the distance in miles means little.

Thoughts and memories pass through the mind as I travel northwards to my new home. A reluctance to travel cannot be entirely good. There is something missing that I need to learn. It is not enough to have emptiness within. "Next the soul must go out," Tauler said; "Go out to the whole world," said Jesus. Perhaps emptiness is necessary if one is really to go out. It may be the first step of the real journey. He travels securely who has nothing, say the French; *sûrement va qui n'a rien.*

51

From the road the Portumna cloister lies in plain view, only a few feet away. This closeness to the road seems somehow a little shocking; the ruins have revealed their secret too soon. The arches are intact on two sides, yet it is much less a place of inwardness and secrecy than was the Kilmallock cloister. Either this cloister has leaked into the world, or the world has leaked into it, but there is almost nothing left here.

I park the Honda and walk around the outside of the ruins, looking for a place to camp. There is a suitable corner at the back, under a tall beech, out of view of the road. Within half an hour the tent is housing me and my goods; I sit here on the meditation stool, sensing the atmosphere of this new place. It is good to feel the presence of a tree overhead. Twenty yards away the Honda leans against another tree, resting after the journey. With its plastic cover reaching to the ground, it looks like a tired old horse just back from the joust and regretting it. We have arrived!

I have been reading a little of the history of this priory. It was originally a Cistercian foundation, established some time before 1254 and dedicated to our Lady. It was taken over by the Dominicans in the early fourteenth century, and they added the names, "St Peter and St Paul". Its full name, then, is "The priory of St Mary and St Peter and St Paul". (It seems I will have to get used to crowds here.) It was the first of the new foundations in Ireland of Blessed Raymond of Capua's reform of the Order. Raymond was confessor to St Catherine of Siena and became Master General of the Order shortly after her death. This reform was greatly needed

after the combined ravages of the Black Death and the Schism of
the fourteenth century. It laid special stress on the liturgy, the
chanting of the divine office in choir and the celebration of High
Mass. Reading about all this in my tent, I wonder whether those
strict men would approve of my present way of life. One way or
the other, I am here; and I doubt that their diet, for example, could
have been stricter than mine — though I fall behind in choral
chanting of the office and High Mass! The priory was suppressed
at the time of the Reformation but was revived in 1640. It was
finally abandoned in the early part of the eighteenth century when
the brethren transferred to Boula, about a mile and a half away.
From 1788 till 1832 it was in use as a Protestant church, and it was
finally abandoned entirely.

But I am looking for an individual story. The individual story,
more than the general one, connects us with a place. I soon find a
moving story about Father Richard O'Madden who was prior of
this community some time in the seventeenth century. His story is
told by his friend Father John O'Heyne, a member of the Athenry
community, who taught philosophy in France and in Louvain.
"Richard O'Madden studied brilliantly in Avila...and came to
Belgium, where he taught at Utrecht. After my first return home
I often heard him preach, and I never heard a more energetic
preacher, neither in our own language nor in any other language
I was acquainted with. He was made Master [the highest academic
distinction in the Dominican Order] in 1678.... On the rout of the
Catholic army in the battle of Aughrim, in 1691, and the plunder-
ing of everything by the victorious enemy, this father hid himself
in an almost impassable bog, where, keeping close during the
fortnight the enemy took to pass, he wasted away through want ...
in the seventieth year of his age."

Another Master (or Meister), Eckhart, spoke movingly of pain
and sorrow, "If it is grievous for the man, it is more so for God."
God suffers in our suffering; "it moves God immeasurably more."
"God suffers it for the sake of some good thing that he has provided
in it for you, and if you will suffer the sorrow that God suffers and

that comes to you through him, it will become godlike — contempt, it may be, just as respect, bitterness just as sweetness, the greatest darkness just as the brightest light."

If Richard O'Madden was not thinking thoughts like this as he died of exposure in a Galway bog, it would surely have comforted him to hear them. If Eckhart is right, then our suffering, like our prayer, lives eternally; it is the suffering of God. Our suffering is perhaps the pains of God's coming to birth in a wicked world.

52

In my childhood there were two elderly itinerant sisters, Bridgie and Jane, who rambled the countryside, calling at favourite houses for food and sometimes lodging. Like comets following elliptical paths of their own, they visited two or three times a year. They never walked together, but in procession. First the dog would arrive, then Bridgie, and five minutes later, Jane. If I think of them now for the first time in years it must be that they remind me of something here. They remind me of my own case. I am arriving in Portumna in procession, not in one piece. That I have been reading about these ruins before looking at them shows that the heart is still in Kilmallock. The mind and body can be transferred with ease from place to place, the mind even more easily than the body, but no one knows how to transfer the heart. It lags behind and keeps its own pace.

When I leave the tent to inspect the ruins I enter first the church, which has a nicely carved doorway. Then to my great disappointment I see that the interior is full of tombstones. There are crowds everywhere here — well, not living people, but crowds even so: the cloister is in full view of every passerby, the choir area is full of tombs, and even the name of the place is a crowd! The choir has a beautiful east window, and I sit on a stone facing it; but I am somehow superfluous there. The place is already full to capacity, and the dead, irritatingly, are able to boast longer residence than the living. They hold their places like irascible Holy Joes. I feel out of it, and I leave within minutes.

There are extensive remains of the living-quarters — some large undefined spaces and many tiny rooms — but they do not speak to me. There are a few doorways, however, and a few narrow windows that are like real 'places', and I stay with them for a while. Doorways and windows, of course, are places of transition, where different worlds meet; so where there is no great difference between inside and outside they lose much of their meaning.

To distract myself from my disappointment with the place, I need to do something practical. I decide to visit a neighbour and ask to fill my water-container. To my surprise, the woman I meet makes it clear by her gestures and her manner of speech that she considers my place on the human scale a very low one, and she directs me accordingly to the tap at a water-trough in the yard. Bridgie and Jane must have experienced this many times in their lives. It is humiliating to be given something that you have neither bought nor received as a gift; it places you by implication in the company of thieves. The rebuff is a little easier to take for being about water, which is the humblest element, always choosing the lowest place. Even if it is not this woman's gift, it is still a gift of the earth, I tell myself. The woman has receded into her house and closed the door decisively. There something is made visible: doors are not only about transition; they are also about exclusion.

Returning to the tent with my gallon of humble water, I reflect that Portumna has already given me a clear theme to meditate on: unwelcome presences. They are everywhere in Portumna, and I am one of them myself!

53

How can emptiness exclude anything? That is what I want to know. How can you welcome emptiness and then want to bolt the door against things you dislike? Surely emptiness welcomes everything. If it does not, then it is not emptiness. It is the ego pretending to be empty. You must go out, said Tauler. But must you let the outside in? Does it come to the same thing? These are thoughts I take with me to my tent tonight.

In the stillness of the night, as happens often, gentler presences come to me as I sit within the tent. Tagore is wise and calm. He knows. "That which oppresses me, is it my soul trying to come out into the open, or the soul of the world knocking at my heart for its entrance?" He asks the question but gives no answer. Perhaps it is wiser to offer no answer to such questions. A question is an ambiguous statement, and the answer removes the ambiguity. In some cases should the ambiguity be left untouched? Yes! It was clear to me even in the first week of this pilgrimage. What resonance there is in ambiguity! I said. Like seashell and eardrum. But now it is not about genteel reflections; it is about general disappointment, depressing tombstones and a surly woman! After a long time of stillness in the tent it is clear that they have to be admitted. Nothing may be excluded for your own convenience.

But is it the end of emptiness when you let everything in? Or could there be just a little emptiness? As in a pot of potatoes! Absurd! The word 'empty' summons up Eckhart, and I cast my mind back over passages I have read and re-read many times. "What is an empty spirit?" he asked. "An empty spirit is one that is confused by nothing, attached to nothing, has not attached its best to any fixed way of acting and has no concern whatever in anything for its own gain, for it is all sunk deep down into God's dearest will and has forsaken its own." I recall a helpful editor who told us that the word translated as "empty" is *ledig* — which can also mean "free". It is not the absence of things (or people or memories) that makes for true emptiness, it is the non-attachment to them even when they are present. In fact the simple absence of something can fill you more than the presence of the same thing ever could: you think about nothing else. Things and people must be allowed in, but they have to be given safe passage through the mind. The self-centred self is a bandit who will leap out from hidden places and take everything "for its own gain." To learn non-attachment is to loose the bandit's hold, to overcome the mindless greed of the self, to give things and people safe passage through the mind, to have "no concern in anything for one's own gain," to see everything as God's own.

Now the next step, at any rate, is clear: you have to let things come to you and do their best or worst, while you stand still and do not waver towards attachment; your spirit must be set so free that it sets free in turn everything it touches. Then you may begin to know a little of what it means to "sink deep down into God's dearest will."

Rain begins to fall, and the sound of its falling on the tent is like a reassurance that God has not forgotten you.

> Lord God, how great you are....
> You stretch out the heavens like a tent.
> Above the rains you build your dwelling.
> You make the clouds your chariot.
> Earth drinks its fill of your gift.

54

The earth smells fresh in the morning, and the sun is shining through thin cloud. There is a lightsome quality about things, absorbed immediately by the mind. Portumna looks a little better in this light. The place has given me nothing, and perhaps that is what I needed most of all: a realistic experience of nothing. It brings to mind a story about a Sufi mystic who lived an itinerant life with his disciples. They would beg their food and lodging wherever they went. This Sufi thanked God continually: "Thank you, God," he would say, "you always give us what we need." In one place they were refused both food and lodging; all day they had nothing to eat and no sheltered place in which to spend the night. Still he continued his prayer, "Thank you, Lord.... " Next day also they were refused food and lodging; every door was closed against them. "Thank you, Lord," he continued to pray. At the end of the third day one of the disciples could stand the contradiction no longer. "Master," he said, "God has given us nothing for the past three days, yet you continue to thank him for giving us everything we need!" "It must be," replied the Sufi, "that we needed three days of poverty, and God has given them to us. Thank you, Lord, you always give us what we need."

After breakfast I make my way to the lake, to pray there. Mediaeval friars lived on fish and vegetables, and for this reason they built their priories, whenever possible, beside a lake or a river. True to custom, the Portumna Priory is no more than a hundred yards from Lough Derg.

Sit at the lake's edge and take your ease.... See the light playing lightly with the tiny waves, bobbing with delight and sliding playfully away on every side with smoothness of inimitable skill. They know nothing of human wilfulness, these waves, this light; nothing of your need to define your life by what you hold your own. They even give and receive their very being in perfect reciprocity.

First the surly woman, take her to your heart, embrace her; whatever in you rejects her is illusory. You have the knowledge of nothingness. You are not a solid Dalton atom resisting all others, knowing nothing of incalculable spaces. Her limitations are yours, plunge them into your own nothingness and dissolve them. Bear her burden in your own being: it is the law of Christ.

And the others, the many from long ago who haunt you still and in your dreams inflict their cruel wounds: boarding school, where almost the only warmth was the heat of anger — the ferocity of teachers, proving to soft country boys the supremacy of violence. Embrace them if you can. You must embrace them. To generations of youths they offered vinegar to drink, a cup of bitter memories. Their joyless lives, like all frail flesh, cruel caricatures of faith, hope and love; try to embrace them. One of them (a quiet one), having no other language, committed suicide; embrace them if you dare. But their subsequent promotion and good standing! Can you embrace them? They impoverished your heart, but you consented cravenly; you are not separate from them. Can you rise up, like the Sufi, and accept your poverty? There is room for them in your emptiness; it can exclude no one. Embrace them in their limitations; they are your own limitations. Stand still and do not waver. Give them now at last safe passage. It is the law of Christ.

In the depths of your cave (said the monk of Spencer Abbey) there can be heard the roar of great waters. They are the tears of the whole world.

55

On the other side of the Shannon in the village of Lorrha lie the ruins of another priory, founded in 1269. I have read that nothing remains except the shell of the church, but since it is only a few miles from here I would like to visit it, at least for an hour or two; and so I set out once more on the Honda. It is a beautiful day and a pleasant journey. The ruins lie close beside the site of the older and very famous Celtic monastery of St Ruadhan of Lorrha. I do not want to give my heart to any of these ruins. There has to be moderation in all things. It is not in fact difficult to hold oneself aloof: lichen-covered tombstones, set at every angle around the priory, are the front line of defence. I will leave them in peace with their property.

The stories of the Dominicans who lived here are brief and similar to one another: studied in Lisbon or Louvain or Paris; taught philosophy or theology there or at home; preached with vigour, was imprisoned, fled or was exiled from the kingdom. Ambrose O'Kennedy taught philosophy in Grenoble, and theology for twenty years in Poitiers. Dominic O'Carroll taught philosophy in Portugal. Anthony O'Carroll, a Master, taught for many years in Lisbon. Another Master, Terence Albert O'Brien, who made a tryst with Ireton, was prior here once. It strikes me very forcibly that all these men I have read about (and countless others like them) were Europeans, while their persecutors were narrowly and self-consciously English. They spoke the languages of Europe, studied and taught there, and felt at ease with its cultures. The notion of Ireland as an inward-looking island community has very shallow roots.

On my way back to Portumna I stop at Friar's Lough. In its depths it conceals the only fire-breathing dragon left in Ireland. Lakes and mountains always hide a secret; this is a quiet and deep lake, a fitting place for a dragon to dwell. In the days when dragons were common, this one was a sore nuisance to the local people; he would raid their farms for cattle and sheep, he would even carry off children to devour them, and in a general way he was wearing out his welcome. The situation was so bad that they had to send for St Patrick. He had, of course, already banished snakes from Ireland; this would complete his clean-up of the country. However, he was now an old man and out of practice in dealing with dragons. He came to the lough and engaged himself straight away in combat with the dragon. The fierce struggle continued for three days, and when St Patrick's strength began to fail he decided to speak to the dragon. "It is a very wrong thing to be fighting; let us reason together," he suggested. The dragon agreed to this; he probably needed a rest himself. St Patrick knew well that the dragon was not gifted with great intelligence, so he said, "If you promise me and these people that you will stay at the bottom of the lake, and that you will never break the surface till Tuesday falls on a Friday, we will leave you alone and in peace." The dragon agreed, and to this day he is waiting at the bottom of the lake for that circumstance to arise.

56

I want to let my community and my family know that I am surviving in the wild, and so I have written some brief letters. Waiting in line in the post office I am conscious of a girl's ear-rings. They are inconspicuous gold ones, noticed only because of our proximity in the queue. They are the cross of Christ, swinging wildly in small arcs as she turns her head to look at this and that. Has any historian marked the year when the cross began to be an ornament? For a few centuries, Christians found it too terrible for visual representation. Crucifixions were still being carried out. If Jesus had been hanged would we have little fourteen-carat scaf-folds dangling from our ears and hanging oh! around our necks? The cross is the central icon of our faith, but it is slipping away by inches to join the dead symbols of forgotten folklores and religions — leprechauns, ankhs and zodiacal signs.

Darkness is falling on the earth — or is it rising out of it? It is evening and there is great silence. The ear-rings trouble me. What is becoming of the cross of Christ? It is our own fault that it is becoming an ornament. We position the cross 'artistically' to balance a flower-pot or to take the bare look off a wall. But the cross is not 'part' of a room; it is not part of any system of relationships. It is an irruption, a scandal, an overturning of every thought and value.

"While the Jews demand miracles and the Greeks look for wisdom, we preach Christ crucified." The flimsy spirituality of growth and self-fulfilment is judged and measured by this; what do growth and self-fulfilment mean when your world is turned upside down by tragedy? In truth, they mean nothing at all. Tell Richard O'Madden about growth and self-fulfilment as he weakens and dies of exposure in a Galway bog. The Christian tradition puts before him the cross of Christ: to remind him of the vulnerability of God, his silent presence in our pain, the tears of the whole world finding their meaning in the heart of Christ. The redemption of human pain! "My God, my God, why have you forsaken me?" — the loneliness and the wonder of the journey to God, over against the hollow decoration and the queue to nowhere.

Christ's life is given for us, he is made sin for us. On the cross he embraced the whole world and its sinfulness, refusing nothing. Every one who dealt violently with him he embraced in return. He did not seek self-fulfilment; "he emptied himself, taking the form of a slave." He is the Place where God is present and plain to be seen. Love is his meaning. That is the law of Christ.

It is now late at night and time to sleep. Lying here in the tent, I think of the Good Friday liturgy. No doubt it was celebrated year after year by those ascetical brethren who lived here. Veneration: how little we know of it! Yet even now it is moving to watch. The hidden cross is uncovered inch by inch. We come and prostrate ourselves before it and plant clumsy kisses on the feet. But however clumsy, it is always moving to watch. It tells how little we know of veneration, how strange to us this warm-blooded custom. It also tells, by the awkwardness of our gestures, how we try to bear our tragedies in isolation.

57

This is the day I leave Portumna. There was no rain last night, and so the tent is dry and can be folded easily. I intend to set out at midday for Athenry. That leaves me with a few hours to take my leave of these ruins and this place. It is pleasant to sit in the cloister and draw one's thoughts together.

I was invaded here, invaded by crowds, crowds of the living and crowds of the dead. Even now as I sit in the cloister I have to greet several passersby whom I have come to know. I have also come to know and accept the present occupants of the choir! The most unwelcome guests were the painful memories of school. Yet I was given the grace to accept all these presences. The empty place for God cannot be locked up; that would be a false emptiness. To be genuine it must be open to the world but somehow not part of the world's logic. "First," said Tauler, "the soul must turn in towards itself." Then "the soul must go out." Since I have a shorter stride than Tauler's I had to discover an intermediate step: the soul must let the outside in. If the door is open, there is sure to be movement both ways, in and out. The essence of emptiness is not a jealously guarded inner space, but *non-attachment* to what comes and goes there. There are two kinds of visitors at the threshold: the welcome and the unwelcome. The usual deal is to bring in the welcome ones and become attached to them, while keeping the others carefully out. I have to welcome them all, and pay them the tribute of non-attachment. Only then can God live in that space and touch with freedom everything I touch.

I was also given a grace to see the cross of Christ. In the solitude of his suffering, the community of the Church was born. He was forsaken by his followers, he even seemed to have been forsaken by his Father; but being lifted up, he drew all things to himself. Better than any other event in history, this shows that there is no contradiction between solitude and community; each needs the other. I have never had longer periods of solitude than during the last five or six weeks, yet I am beginning to discover a deeper meaning in the Church, the community of the faithful. I am to embrace them all: love your friends and your enemies, living and dead.

By learning to let the outside reach in, I may learn next to reach out. I know in advance that I can reach out to others only if I reach from emptiness; reaching from my ego will do them no good at all. I looked through the works of a spiritual writer who opposes 'introvert' spirituality to 'extravert', proclaiming the latter as the good news for today. That is a false opposition, like opposing one lobe of your brain to the other. "With every creature," said Meister Eckhart (a more reliable guide), "the more it indwells in itself, the more it gives itself out.... The masters say no creature has such close indwelling in itself as body and soul, yet nothing has such a great sallying-forth as the soul in her highest part." I picture it this way: a book protrudes over the edge of a table; the more it reaches in, the more it is able to reach out. If it reaches out farther than it reaches in, it will topple over the edge. Even in your reaching out, stand still and do not waver from your emptiness.

Soon the Honda is loaded and ready for the journey. She will not be sorely taxed today; the distance to Athenry is about thirty-five miles. After a mile or two I notice that she has picked up another attention-seeking trick: when I sound the horn she stops dead, like a good dog coming to heel. But I can outwit her any day, as St Patrick outwitted the dragon: I will sound the horn again when Tuesday falls on a Friday.

58

My visit to Athenry will be a brief pause in the journey to Connemara, where I intend to stay for the remainder of my pilgrimage. I will finish as I began: far away from towns and villages, near water if possible, in the deepest solitude, where I can pray with the Church. My heart is already set on it.

It is early afternoon when I reach the small town of Athenry. The first large structure to be seen is the ruined Dominican Priory, as an exceedingly friendly old lady assures me. Oh yes indeed, she says, the Dominicans were associated with Athenry for more than six hundred years; very proud of it we are. She has already noted the antiquity of the Honda and the battered lantern at the back, and this may be what causes her to mention the antiquity of the Dominican connection. And she is quite old herself. We are a community of ancients. As I leave her, she is nodding and beaming a beautiful smile, outclassing with the greatest of ease her opposite number in Portumna.

From the road, the ruins look majestic, on a larger scale than any of the others I have seen. *Splendidum coenobium*, de Burgo called it. This was once a great centre of study and preaching; and with Portumna it was a strong centre of Blessed Raymond's Reform in Ireland. O'Heyne, himself a member, lists thirty-two members of the community, though at the time of his writing in 1706 they had been dispersed. Many lived in exile in various European cities, and others were dying in English prisons. Many others had been put to death. The story follows the familiar pattern.

I camp quickly and spend an hour resting; it is also a time to read a little about the past of this ancient great centre. Where is the individual story that will connect me with it? A namesake, Donagh, was put to death some time after 1651, but nothing is told of his life. Redmond O'Kenny, "at least ninety years of age, was left in Ireland by the Protestants because of the infirmity of old age, though evicted from his priory." He had studied in Spain and had "ministered with zeal and success among the people for about sixty years." If I meet the little old lady again I will tell her about him! Pierce Kenna preached in the neighbourhood for twenty-four years, received at least eighteen young men into the Order, and was once Prior of Kilmallock. John O'Quillan, "always contented with poor garments," was so talented (*tantopere ingenio valuit*) that he mastered almost all the sciences without a teacher. Captured by the Cromwellians he was decapitated, his head fixed on a spike and exposed as a trophy.

With that gruesome image I have as much as I can bear at present, and I put the book away. It is wrong to recall the past unless it be to redeem it. It presents so many real and imagined reasons for resentment. We have to embrace it or it destroys us. Many things in our past, as a people, have undermined confidence and impoverished the heart, but (like the Sufi) we have to embrace that poverty to redeem it. Bitter memories must be drained to the dregs or they become a poison in the cup. If we recall them it must be to a mind that sees the ultimate meaning of history as a struggle towards God, and to a heart that relates them consciously to the cross of Christ.

59

"In consideration that the monasterie or house of ffriars of Athenrie is situated amongst the Irishry and that by the dissolution thereof, our sovereign lord shoulde have lyttle or no profit ... the saide house of ffriars shall stand without dissolucion." In 1541 the friars of Athenry petitioned not to be suppressed and their petition was granted — Henry VIII's motives for suppressing monasteries being made quite clear in the process! The smiling old lady was right about the six centuries of Dominican presence.

Meyler de Bermingham, a Norman lord, brought the Domincans to Athenry in 1241. (I am reading that book again!) His and the de Burgo family were generous patrons for centuries, and the priory church became a favourite burial place for their descendents, even up to the present century. I beg just one last benefit from them, that they should not occupy the choir, if possible. Please!

To gain access to the ruins I have to find Christy Barrett who holds the key. He invites me into his house and introduces his wife. They are so gracious that I am made to feel I am doing them an honour by visiting them. "Are there tombstones in the choir?" I ask. Yes, a couple of big ones and several smaller ones. Big ones? Yes, enormous. This is a sharp disappointment, but at least I am

prepared for the worst. After an hour I leave the smiling couple and
make my way to the ruins.

It is worse than I could ever have imagined. Right in the centre
of the choir area is a gigantic structure in hideous pseudo-classical
style, adorned with meaningless pillars and steps and stone-
worked drapery, surmounted twenty feet above by a foolish-
looking urn. The one point in its favour is its poor state of repair.
It is so fatuous in its conception that it makes death look obscene,
the empty urn on top expressing nothing — just vacuity. There is
no religious symbol of any kind, no affirmation of anything but the
shabby after-life of the ego. It does not even have the minimal
grace to be on a small scale; it tries to dominate by the sheer self-
assertion of its bulk. I find myself tingling with rage at its presence,
as many must have done before me. The most maddening thing
about it is its total insensitivity to the place in which it stands; it is
related to nothing but itself. In its way it is perfect: it is a perfect
image of the human ego.

I pray as much as my anger will allow me for the people who
lie buried within it (it is not their fault); and then I leave quickly.
It has ruined this place for meditation, dominating every perspec-
tive. The fine window of the choir cannot be seen without its
graceless bulk getting in the way. Would that Henry VIII could
come back for five minutes and dissolve it!

60

It is now late evening and I sit enclosed in the tent; through the
flaps the battered lantern offers sufficient light by which to write.
I can think of nothing but that repulsive monument. How can I,
how can anyone, be so angry about blocks of limestone and slabs
of marble? It must symbolise other things. It symbolises, I think,
the ego; and other people's egos are always ugly!

The cult of the self in much of modern psychology is in practice the cult of the ego, despite the theoretical distinctions that are sometimes made. This 'self', if it is to merit so much devotion, has to be thought of as good, even the highest good. I once came on an amazing statement taken from *The International Encyclopaedia of Psychiatry, Psychology, Psychoanalysis and Neurology*: "Man is basically constructive, accepting, creative, spontaneous, open to experience, self-aware and self-realizing. It is parental, societal and cultural controls, through manipulation of rewards and threats of punishment, which inhibit the otherwise natural development of self-expression and self-actualization." It shows a silly Romanticism in regard to children (and noble savages), but it is a formula for the destruction of all family and social structures — and therefore also of children. Nevertheless, like an advertisement for supermarket foods, it touts itself in a language of bland and cloying affirmation. "Natural development of self-expression and self-actualization" reads like a cereal packet. As Peggy Rosenthal remarked, there is "a warm glowing sense of sun-ripened natural goodness." She ferrets out a gem from Abraham Maslow: "To be natural and spontaneous, to know what one is, and what one really wants, is a rare and high culmination that comes infrequently, and that usually takes long years of courage and hard work." In her brilliant gladiatorial style (in *Words and Values*) she does full justice to the absurdity of talking about self-absorption in the traditional language of self- denial. The self can do no wrong, they seem to say. "When an activity feels as though it is valuable or worth doing," wrote Carl Rogers, "it is worth doing." It seems likely that this extremism is a reaction to a previous extremism that saw human nature as totally corrupt.

When all of this is taken up by Christian writers and teachers, and is given back to us under a veneer of spirituality, it is (like the pseudo-classical tomb) very maddening. Modern psychology is itself a pseudo-classic: what does it care that *psyche* used to mean soul? When it plants itself in holy places it usually only spoils them for meditation. The choir, the Holy of Holies, the place where

God's praise should rise up, is filled with the vulgar forms of the ego.

I have blown out the lantern. Lying now in darkness I think about the two ways: the way of psychology and the way of spirituality. And I am suddenly and chillingly aware of the danger of missing both of them, suspecting the one and falling short of the other.

61

Anthony the Great, 'the Father of Monks', spent twenty years in complete solitude in the desert. He wrestled incessantly with demons, and gave detailed advice on how to deal with them: "how to recognise their traits: for example, which of them is less wicked, and which more; and in what kind of pursuit each of them exerts himself, and how each of them is overturned and expelled." As the years went by, many Christians came to know of him, and began to imitate his way of life. In the year 305 A.D. he came out of solitude to be their spiritual father. Once, he visited a populous town, and his disciples tried to protect him from the crush of people; but he told them to be at ease: "These are no more numerous than those demons with whom we wrestle on the mountain!"

His methods were the exact opposite of introspective psychological ones: a modern person would say he projected everything shamelessly outwards. Yes, but it was certainly one way of keeping the inner being spotless. It was not a form of alienation or a refusal of responsibility; on the contrary, the man was hard at work every day, doing battle with his demons; and the battle was for his spiritual life. Modern people in therapy sometimes do battle with pillows, but pillows could never be more than a pale imitation of Anthony's demons. There is little of interest that can be said about their various traits or about the pursuits they exert themselves in, or how they are to be overturned and expelled.

As I prepare to leave for Connemara I am conscious that I will probably have to face some demons in that great solitude. Let it be! I may be able to scare them off by threatening to embrace them! I may develop a *Plutonic* relationship with them! They are very cowardly, Anthony said; it is because they are powerless (and know it) that they have to come in numbers and disguise themselves. Very well, let them come in numbers, and see if I can guess their names.

Part Three

62

Once again we are on the road, the ancient Honda and myself, travelling westwards through Oranmore to Galway city, then north-west along by Lough Corrib to Oughterard and Maam Cross, westwards again in sight of the Twelve Pins to Ballinahinch and finally to our destination, Toombeola. It means "Beola's tumulus", according to P. W. Joyce, who wrote about it in 1869. "This Beola, who was probably an old Firbolg chieftan, is still vividly remembered in tradition; and a remarkable person he must have been, for the place of his internment is also commemorated, namely Toombeola." The Firbolg were a pre-Celtic race, dark and short, unlike the Celts who were tall with red-blond hair. This neighbourhood seems to be a place of long memories — a perfect condition for demons to come out into the open. Perhaps some of them are Firbolg!

I passed Toombeola and was well on the way to Roundstone before I realised my mistake and turned back. Even the leisurely pace of the Honda is a little out of scale with this landscape; we will both have to become attuned to slower paces. There is little in Toombeola to fix it on any road-map — there is a bridge and two or three houses — but then maps are abstract, while Toombeola is full of what the mediaevals called *haecceitas*, a coined word meaning *this-ness*, simple particularity. Cities and towns are full of signs, things that refer you to other things; in that sense a city or a town is a kind of language. But Toombeola is a place of silence; everything is just what it is and nothing else. It is a place of simple essences. The structure of the earth itself, its skeleton, seems to jut out: for miles in every direction there are long ridges of rock as well as clusters and individual rocks dropped by glaciers in the unimaginably distant past. The landscape is a patchwork of rocky ridge and sea-inlet, marshy bogland, moor and freshwater lake, very restful to the eye.

After detailed enquiries and much searching along laneways

and through tiny uneven fields I come to the site of the fifteenth century priory. There is a small roofless structure there, but it is post-Dominican, as my book tells me. "In this priory ... there were generally eight religious; but from the beginning of the reign of Elizabeth it was not inhabited"; all the stones were removed to build a castle in the neighbourhood. The site is now a cemetery overgrown with high grass, weeds and furze, very difficult to penetrate. Compared to this utterly silent place, other cemeteries seem wide awake and fussy, almost as if the people there were not really dead. This may well be the quietest place on earth. Typically, it is close to water: it could scarcely be nearer to the edge of a narrow sea-inlet. A few paces from the cemetery, under a scraggy thornbush, the tent-pole is already raised, and one sets about the practical business of living.

63

It is as if God forgot to put this place in motion. Silence seems to sing here, and everything stands in a vast stillness of night — an essential stillness equalled only by the dead. They, the silent neighbours, even celebrate their feast with silence: it is All Souls' Night. Frost gives the air a crystalline quality and you look up in wonder at the million white cities, "bright boroughs", and the immeasurable spaces between them. The gulf of space is terrible if you try to hold a little space in safety for yourself. Give yourself away, empty fugitive! There is nothing to hold, nothing ... you can hold nothing.... You look into the abyss of space to see what an abyss is like. *He* is the abyss who overflows his creation. Words of St Augustine come to you:

> Lord ... you have no need to be contained in anything;
> is it because you contain

all things in yourself and fill them?
The things which you fill
do not sustain and support you,
as water-vessels support the liquid which fills them.
Even if they were broken to pieces,
you would not flow out of them and away.

As the hours follow one another, starlight shimmers on the water and the light of God's saints irradiates the mind, catching its small waves. God is in all things, they keep repeating. God is in all things, said Meister Eckhart.

God is in all things.
The more he is in things,
the more he is out of things:
the more in the more out,
and the more out the more in.

He is not contained in them as water is contained in a jar. It is the other way around, as St Augustine said. Imagine a jar in the ocean; it is filled with water but it does not contain the ocean. That is very clear. Still, every metaphor fails: the ocean fills the empty space within the jar, yes, but it does not fill the space occupied by the walls of the jar. Eckhart follows this metaphor, as he always does, to the point where it fails, and says that the union of God and the creature is closer than any kind of union of material substances; it is a complete inwardness or intimacy to each other. God is in the creature and the creature in God. "In spiritual matters, the one is always completely in the other.... With a spiritual vessel, whatever is received is in the vessel, and the vessel in it."

The more he is in things, the more he is out of things. There is no intimacy without the beyond, no immanence without transcendence. In practice it means that there is no possibility of private depth, no God in the pocket. In prayer you are not sinking into self-absorption, cultivating certain feelings, polishing the ego till it seems to shine. Instead you are face to face with the transcendent

God who overflows all creatures. Even if your vessel (your power to contain, your ego) is "broken to pieces," as St Augustine said, God is not lost. He contains all things; you may even be as useful to him broken as whole.

The eternal silence of the infinite spaces filled Pascal with terror. "The finite is annihilated in the presence of the infinite," he wrote, "and becomes pure nothingness." At that moment he must have been concentrating on the words *annihilated* and *nothingness*, and not hearing the word *presence*.

But Eckhart maintained the two poles of the paradox: the more out the more in.... God is out of things; he is like Nothing, he said — like total absence. But he is simultaneously total presence.

64

Let everything that lives and that breathes
give praise to the Lord. Alleluia!

These are the last words of the Book of Psalms (they are perhaps the last word in every sense). The final psalms in the book are shouts of praise to God, and it would not disturb my silent neighbours in the cemetery if I shouted them at the top of my voice. But we bring our inhibitions with us into the wilderness, so I mutter them under my breath instead! I am praying the Morning Office at the mouth of my tent, and I am conscious that at the deepest level I am not alone. I cannot believe that my deceased neighbours would feel excluded by the phrase, "everything that lives and that breathes." They live and breathe eternity. Eckhart's words would make them feel especially included: "The time that passed away a thousand years ago is now as present and as near to God as this very instant."

In reality, then, I have a large choir praising God with me this morning. They are the adepts and I am lagging behind, enfeebled by the complications of the twentieth century. Thomas Merton acknowledged the difficulty we have in praising anything today: "Praise is cheap.... Everything is praised. Soap, beer, tooth-paste, clothing, mouthwash, movie stars, all the latest gadgets which are supposed to make life more comfortable — everything is constantly being 'praised'. Praise is now so overdone that everybody is sick of it, and since everything is 'praised' with the official hollow enthusiasm of the radio announcer, it turns out in the end that nothing is praised. Praise has become empty.... Are there any superlatives left for God? They have all been wasted on foods and quack medicines ... "

The wilderness is surely the place to learn praise. In the absence of useless products I may learn to praise God for himself.

> Praise God in his holy place,
> praise him in his mighty heavens.
> Praise him for his powerful deeds,
> praise his surpassing greatness ....
> Let everything that lives and that breathes
> give praise to the Lord. Alleluia!

65

The mediaevals defined time as "the measure of motion", suggesting a uniformity that is certainly absent from the *experience* of time. I embarked on this pilgrimage to meditate on time and place; but drawing near now to the end, I can still make no definition of time. That does not bother me: meditation is not really concerned with definitions but with experiencing realities in all their untidiness. I have experienced time flowing at greatly different speeds. Days and nights passed slowly at first in Toombeola, then more and more quickly. There is probably some kind of 'inner clock' which does not run at a uniform speed as outer clocks do. When it is running quickly, outer events seem slow by comparison; but when it slows down, outer events seem to pass by at great speed — there are more of them per 'inner minute'. The inner clock seems to be almost stopped at present, and so the days and nights race past.

This image of 'inner clock' might also shed light on the varying speed of time from childhood to old age: compared with the bird-like speed of a child's mind, outer events seem almost eternal; but when the inner clock slows down with age, life seems to pass by with alarming speed. (Is it too fanciful to think that when the inner clock stops completely — in death? — all events will appear to be happening in a single instant?)

Place is easier to think about than time. We are even inclined to think of time in terms of place: days could be neighbouring boxes, as on a calendar; years are visualised as following one another in a line; and we say *always* for *all times*, *thereafter* when we mean something like *thenafter*, and *before* (meaning in front of) for *earlier*. Place is so easy (we have chosen to regard it as more intelligible because it is visible) that we can express just about any inner state in terms of it. In future times when I want to visualise peace I will think of this place: my name for peace will be Toombeola.

There are plenty of precedents in the Scriptures for locating inner states on an outer map. As the Hebrews wandered for years through the desert they suffered severe hardships; in one place they grumbled so much against Moses that he named the place 'Trial' and 'Contention' (*Massah* and *Meribah*), because "they put God on trial by saying, 'Is he with us or not?'" Anthony of the Desert, too, placed his demons on a kind of map; he saw them outside himself. There is a great deal of wisdom in plotting the inner life on an outer map. The day when a deep friendship began can be named 'Friendship Day' and its anniversary celebrated every year. The day when God did something special in one's life, and even the place, can be marked on the map. Naming things makes them more visible and easier to find again. They become signposts along the way; and like signposts, they enable one to stop going around in circles, repeating the same mistakes, wandering in a nameless wilderness forever. The greater the wilderness, the greater the need for signposts and maps.

O that today you would listen to his voice!
Harden not your hearts as at Meribah,
as on that day at Massah in the desert
when your fathers put me to the test;
when they tried me, though they saw my work.

66

St Athanasius, who wrote the life of Anthony, does not say that Anthony banished his demons. He contended with them, and he gradually learned to *understand* them. The demonic, says Rollo May, is "any natural function which has the power to take over the whole person." It could be sex, he adds, or anger, or rage, or the craving for power. The notion of little demons fluttering around in the air and trying to gain entry was "a deteriorated form of the concept", and was rightly thrown out in the Enlightenment and the Age of Reason. However, as he wisely adds, "in discarding the false 'demonology', we accepted, against our intention, a banality and a shallowness in our whole approach to mental disease." In throwing out our demons we threw out our angels as well; and far from being freed and filled with enlightenment, we are delivered over to apathy.

The angels and demons in Rollo May's picture are aspects of the self. But our century has seen forces of evil that are larger than the individual self, and are often, in fact, called 'demonic'. We feel helpless to banish them, and we cannot ignore them. Are we to embrace them? I think we should embrace them with the mind: we should try to understand them, which is what Anthony did.

I am a little disappointed that my demons are not showing their faces. They come in numbers, Anthony said, and in disguise. Are they lurking somewhere? The demon of Fear did not approach even as I slept near this lonely cemetery on All Souls' Night. And I cannot see it anywhere in disguise. Loneliness has not visited me, nor any other demon, whether aspects of the self or not. Where is everybody? Where are the Firbolg? There are not even wild beasts, the companions of demons in the Scriptures. The only beasts I see this afternoon are a couple of particularly lazy cows in a little field nearby. They lie there for hours, peacefully chewing the cud, their inner clocks probably almost stopped. They are letting me see that the most important business in the world is to ruminate!

67

All night long a hard wind blew in from the sea, and the tent flapped noisily, like a giant bird trying to rise into the air. Eight more pegs were needed to secure it to the ground. In the hour before dawn the wind bore heavy rain, which it flung with all its force against the trembling tent. Slower, heavier drops fell from the thornbush above me, but not a drop of water entered. On such a night a tent is tested to its limit.

In the morning, drops fall in little companies, now and again, from the overhanging thornbush, and the wind blows in periodic gusts; the world is dry sobbing at the end of its tantrum. Peeping out from the tent I have the impression that here I have all the *this-ness* I am ever likely to want! The narrow path beside me (it is the path to the cemetery) has puddles of water along its whole length.

The small area of the tent, it seems, is the only dry place on earth. The rain held off during breakfast but now it is beginning to fall again. My life today will be a narrowly confined one.

"The more the soul is collected, the narrower she is, and the narrower the wider," said Eckhart. At first the spiritual path seems narrow and constricting: you think only of what you are missing. Then as you stay on the path it opens out to include the whole world.

Recently the Meister shapes all my thoughts. "Love is quite bare, quite pure, quite detached in itself," he said — words that suit the mood of this morning's weather! Yet this is how he began to speak of the universality of love. Confined in this narrow place, I would like to hear something about universality! Let me listen. "Love is quite bare, quite pure, quite detached." In other words, love is love and not something else: by 'pure' he means something like *chemically pure*, by 'bare' he means, I suppose, *undisguised*, and by 'detached' he means *unmixed with other attitudes* such as greed or the need to control. If the love in you is "pure, bare and detached" — if it is love and not something else posing as love — you are like a fountain that pours itself out without measure. (The moment the fountain begins to calculate the returns, it is no longer a fountain but a drain.) You are a child of your Father who sends rain on the just and the unjust and makes the sun to rise on the evil and on the good alike. If the love in you is that kind of love, then "it is a certain truth that all the virtuous deeds performed by all people are yours as perfectly as if you had performed them yourself, and even purer and better." It matters little in itself whether the virtuous deed came into existence through you or through another. The goodness that came into existence through you belongs to others, and the goodness that came into existence through others belongs as much to you as if you had brought it into existence yourself — if you do not separate yourself from them. But the moment you separate yourself, there is mine and yours, and therefore competition. Do not only bear one another's burdens; bear one another's virtues, one another's joy, one another's goodness. The existence of Christian community depends on a universal kind of love.

All day long the rain has continued to fall, and in the afternoon I am still "bounded in a nutshell," enclosed in the small space of the tent. By four o'clock the light is beginning to fail. The world seems a narrow place; it neither smiles nor speaks to me of anything, and for this I have been waiting long. Like all living things, love grows in particular places.

68

A week later the weather has cleared and the world is full of cold brightness every day. You have tried to reach out and remember everyone you ever knew, to give them safe passage through the mind, making their goodness yours and your goodness theirs. You have tried to imagine the suffering of the whole world, relating it to the cross of Christ, and praying for the resurrection which has happened and is forever still to happen. You have tried to praise God without the interference of the ego. But all your efforts are puny and intermittent; the least thing can distract you. Sit still, it is Christ who prays in you for the whole world. Go into the heart of Christ, the Holy of Holies, and there you will see all things related to the Father.

In a few days my pilgrimage will have come to an end, and a new (or rather an old) restlessness is beginning to make itself felt. I am sitting at the mouth of the tent, persuading myself to sit still for the present. There is no need to go anywhere yet. This is the centre of the world, the navel. I remember seeing, in the ruins of ancient Rome, a low circular structure called *umbilicus orbis*, the navel of the world. It was considered the central point of the Roman Empire, and therefore the hub of the world. Tourists would stand on it and imagine that for one minute they were at the centre of all things. The ancient Romans did not know that the world was more or less a sphere. Every point on its surface is the centre; every person in the world is standing at the centre. The pole of my tent here in Toombeola is planted on the central point of the world. In fact it is impossible to waver from the centre.

I remember (it is a time for remembering) the delighted account of the first men to fly over the North Pole. They made a large circle to be sure of taking in the Pole. "We thus made a non-stop flight around the world in a few minutes," wrote Richard Byrd. "In doing that we lost a whole day in time, and of course when we completed the circle we gained that day back again. Time and direction became topsy-turvy at the Pole. When crossing it on the same straight line, we were going north one instant and south the next. No matter how the wind strikes you at the North Pole it must be travelling north, and however you turn your head you must be looking south." They conveyed an excitement like that of little boys playing with a ball, the ball in this case being the world itself.

No pilot would look down in excitement at Toombeola. It is remote from cities and excitement. But it is nonetheless a centre of the world. "Where I am, there is God," said Eckhart. Every place is south of here and all winds blow in this direction. "What you sought before now seeks you, and what you fled from now flees from you." If God cannot be found in this place he cannot be found anywhere. "You need not seek God here or there," he said, "he is not further than the door of your heart."

The people of Toombeola would understand him perfectly, I think, for there is an old saying, a *seanfhocal*, that says "God's help is nearer than the door": *is gaire cabhair Dé ná an doras.*

69

There is greater sadness in leaving a desolate place than in leaving a city; one's attachment to a city is often to its superficial detail, but only essential attachments are possible in a wilderness. All morning there has been a sense of mournful leavetaking. Never till now have I felt sad at leaving a mean thornbush, or an overgrown cemetery, or a sedgy headland.

'Toombeola' will mean peace: not the peace that comes when everything is excluded, but the peace when everything is included. Lest I should ever in future times be tempted to search for a private God, Meister Eckhart warns, "Whoever loves God as he ought, must love others as himself, rejoicing in their joys as in his own joys, and desiring their honour as much as his own honour, and loving the stranger as one of his own."

> For you shall go out in joy,
> And be led forth in peace.

Joy is the fruit of deep soil, but it must go out, it cannot stop itself from going out. Peace, like any plant, must go out from the rich darkness of the earth; love and freedom must go out. In a word, the soul must go out. That is not an irksome task; they find joy in meeting the world. Love is not the enemy of law, freedom delights to express itself in commitment, joy brims over into work and play. Their truth lies in the mutuality of inner and outer. They want to leap into the world and gallop against the wind towards their farthest limits. Poets impose on themselves the strictest measures of rhythm and metre; and their ink does not find its freedom in the bottle but by laying itself out indelibly on the page. *For you shall go out in joy* ... It is not a flight *from* freedom but *into* freedom. "You ought not to flee or deny or suspect your own inwardness," said the Meister, "you should learn to work in it and with it and from it, so that you can transform inwardness into activity and bring your activities into your inwardness, and so that you can learn to train yourself to act in freedom."

70

Geographically I am about to complete a circle: I am returning to Ennismore from where I set out three months ago. In sadness and joy I fold up the tent and prepare for the long journey home.

It is the first Sunday of Advent, a good day for beginnings and endings. The Liturgy conveys a sense of an old world ending and a new world beginning. An end that was only an end would be annihilation; you believe in the Lord of life, and the end can never be the end. Only a *beginning* can be an end!

"The soul must go out; it must travel away from itself, above itself." But it must never leave the centre; indeed, it cannot leave — because every place in the world is the centre, every moment a sacrament of eternity.

In the heart of every man and woman you meet you will reach out to the centre of creation and touch eternity — if you do not waver from your emptiness.

"For your house is the last before infinity, whoever you are."